Any and Every Indian's Guide to The Chinese Economic Miracle

Role of Civilization, Culture and Society in Economic Growth

Siba Prasad Dasgupta
Susmita Dasgupta

Any and Every Indian's Guide to
The Chinese Economic Miracle

A Susmita Dasgupta Presentation

Contents

Preface

The author of this book is my father who turns eighty this October. He has been a formidable student in his times but opted for the corporate sector rather than academia because of the higher salaries and glamour of the former and the decided lack of either in the latter. He comes from a family of academicians and his was an age of the rising individualism; it was considered to be more fashionable and meritorious to move away from inherited occupations and strike out on one's own into uncharted territories. The original manuscript that my father wrote was an enormous sheaf. It contained many details of the Chinese policies. The reading was good but the matter did not conclude anywhere; besides there were many authors who wrote copiously on China with a similar lack of conclusion. These books, including my father's original manuscript tried to explain China's growth post facto in the language of economic theories derived from the West and contextualised in the development of the Western capitalism.

Reading through these published works, I felt that China's growth lay neither in its policies, nor in its politics, neither in its institutions or the lack of it and nor in the form of its government. China grew through a revolutionary organisation of its family, social, cultural and community capital and the Chinese growth was an impulse from below and not a set of decisions from above. It was a people's movement and not a government's effort because when Mao decided to impose growth from above he landed China into the world's worst ever famine but when Deng decided to release that stranglehold, forces of prosperity were released. The Chinese knew how to form groups and much like the rock bands of America, the Chinese bands were dedicated to manufacturing enterprise and innovation. The street corner clubs were hubs of investments and production; family ties and networks were channels of trade and finance. It was through the use of human and social capital that China grew.

The Chinese growth is also ridden with conflict; namely the tussle between the large corporations and the rock band like manufacturing teams and there was also a tussle between the public sector enterprises and the departments in the government that administered them and not to speak of the conflict between the private and public sector economic giants. The Chinese have shown little respect for the so-called "nation" because communities sabotaged city companies and the city based corporations tried every means to displace the communities. Corruption, murders, encounters rocked the Chinese growth story shredding to smithereens the hunky dory dream of the Chinese nationalism. China grew just because the people know how to combine forces and what to combine them for and for the Chinese, innovation of high tech products is an aspiration rather than to be able to consume and show these products off.

The present book is therefore as much a treatise on the Chinese sociology and history as it is a story of China's economic policies. It shows, as no book before it has revealed, the role of the social capital in the form of family and community ties, neighbourhood groups and kinship networks in pulling off an economic growth which today appears to the world at large as the Chinese miracle!

Susmita Dasgupta
New Delhi, 2014

Chapter One

Why Does China Intrigue Us

China interests us because of its grand paradox. One the one hand we have its spectacular growth while on the other, we observe its non-democratic government which does not always follow the western paradigm of rational modernity. With mind-sets trained to regard economic growth as possible only through the capitalist path based upon liberal governments and democratic politics, China's growth emanating from a communist system with little individual freedom and undeveloped markets and modern financial institutions seems to be an anomaly. While we would love to be a part of the Chinese growth story yet China's poor human rights records, queer institutions of justice and jurisprudence and the utter disregard of democratic opinions scares us. It is always more likely that a country which is so disproportionately rich will dictate the ways of the world and force nations to retreat from democracy and modern forms of governance. Among democracies such as India's and liberal societies of the West, the Chinese spectacle brings some trepidation along with eager anticipation. What does China's growth mean for the world at large? Would the proliferation of opportunities offered by the Chinese growth colonize the world at the hands of this draconian dragon nation? Would this mean that the Chinese system shall prevail over systems protecting individual freedom and liberty?

The Chinese growth is based on a gargantuan expansion of its manufacturing might. It makes China consume and command over half of the global natural resources like iron ore, coal, copper, nickel, and platinum and so on. If the world produces some 1500 million tonnes of finished steel in a year, then China produces around 700 million tonnes of that. If the total gold production of the world in 2012 has been 2690 tonnes, then China imported 30% of the total production. Of the total trade of 1000 million tonnes of iron ore in 2012, China imported around 60% of the same. The story of other minerals and metals are pretty close. Many countries including India are on the anvil of becoming pure mineral exporters because of the pull of the demand for these raw materials by China. Currencies across the developing nations have plummeted because none can withstand the competition from the Chinese factories, while China buys up the debt instruments in the USA and EU leave these nations badly indebted to China leaving very little room for the recovery from chronic recession. China today has the power to crush the first world and colonize the third world. This makes China a giant power that no one seems to have any power to confront. China will alone call the shots not only in international diplomacy but also in the economies of individual nations.

India's anxiety in tapping its natural resources, the pressures that are exerted by foreign capital to access its minerals like iron ore, coal and bauxite and the slow but steady compromises on democratic rights of indigenous people and the farmers in protecting their lands against forceful acquisitions are driven mainly by the fact that we are unable to compete with the Chinese imports and are increasingly using our natural resources to pay for the import of manufactures. The Chinese growth is breaking autarkies in economies and sovereignty among nations. The Chinese growth is rapid, rabid and in some cases rapacious.

China today has formidable trade surpluses with the world's largest economies namely the United States, European Union and Japan. It is the world's largest exporter of goods and services and the second largest importer of manufactured goods. China has captured almost the entire markets of these nations with cheap manufactures. The huge trade surpluses have been used to buy off debt instruments of these countries as a result of which China can today dictate both economic policies and strategic decisions almost across the entire developed world. The economic prowess today threatens to change the power relations across the world, making China so powerful a country that no one dares to criticize its utter abrogation of human rights and its high handedness over Tibet and posturing in Central Asia and in the South China Sea. The last mentioned factors make it difficult for the rest of the humanity outside China to be too pleased with the Chinese growth, for it is a growth that will render democracies and humanitarianism and the countries supporting them as unimportant.

In the popular mind, China is a vast country with high

population concentrated around the rude mountains off Manchuria and Mongolia, dry and cold windswept Gobi desert, some thickly populated rice growing river delta, some obscure sea coasts full of poor and hungry people. China is seen as an unfree society run by Communist bosses, and with a panoptic State that denies even the most obvious citizen rights. The economic growth of China is therefore as much of a welcome makeover from this dreary image but also scary because China's rules appear mindless, its ethics confusing, punishments cruel and justice obscure. Life out in China is dark and dingy, cramped and covert and yet this country is likely to dominate the civilized world.

Most of the world construes China as a poor and underdeveloped country that has seemed to suddenly wake up to the worship of Mammon. When compared to India, often known as its twin in terms of population and poverty and state of underdevelopment, China's achievements prove a point for those who advocate that it is possible for countries to emerge out of poverty by adopting market friendly policies especially those devised by the International Monetary Funds with a series of deregulations and privatizations. But looked at carefully, the story is not quite this. China's growth story has proved to the world that individualistic capitalism supported by liberal states is not the only way to develop; China's communist and closed regimes, more of custom based than rule based society and a communitarian approach to capital accumulation can actually produce growths that are more gigantic than those which are possible out of the Western model. Chinese growth model is far from the typical European model and clearly tells us that there are other ways to reach the top without toeing the Western line. For long the world has searched for an alternative growth path; happily China has been able to show that to us.

If we marvel today at China's unstoppable economic progress and wonder how the sleeping mass of ineffectual and passive people known for shoddy technological development, little artistry and absolutely no refinement for democratic political institutions could suddenly awaken to such miraculous proportions so as to be able to hold economies of advanced nations to ransom, then we are just being ignorant. For most of the world's written history China has led mankind's economic progress, been one of the first people to have a state system, an organized bureaucracy and invented the competitive examinations for civil services as early as 3 BCE ! China also has been a home to almost all the inventions we use today, namely silk, ink, and paper, printing press, glass, mirror and gun powder. China has known the art of floriculture far ahead of the rest of mankind; it developed an elaborate system of medicine, excelled in botany, created new plant species. It had an advanced art market and its elite often collected archaeological remains to enhance social status. Indeed, looking back on prehistory, China seems to have been home to the Peking Man and then to homo sapiens who developed settled farming again ahead of the rest of the world. China's technology of bronze casting and steel making took place centuries before it developed anywhere else. By the beginning of the middle Ages, China had the ore smelters and the blast furnace which appeared in Europe only a millennium later. Changa'an was the place in China from which the Silk Route originated as China's silk paved the way for one of the longer regimes of global trade across Central Asia that connected the worlds of Europe and Asia.[1]

China has been the seat of major technological innovations; wheel, wheel barrow, pulley, row cultivation, gun powder, blast furnaces to make steel, glass, mirror, paper, printing, and of silk and woven silk. Advances in such areas helped China not only dominate the world externally but also grow as a self-sufficient economy. Economic powers of China have often been the reasons for the country's aggression and expansionism; its military aggression being closely connected to the needs of managing the economic surplus, much like the present times. Patterns those have obtained in China as a part of its economic growth in recent decades are continuities from its past. It will not be an exaggeration to say China has always been a world leader in economy, polity and technology. China's present growth impetus is its determination to always be a world leader, with China as the Middle Kingdom with the Heaven above and the nether below and all other kingdoms and empires as minute tributaries to its greatness upon earth! China's civilizational position was interrupted by only a brief spell of colonialism in the aftermath of the opium war; its subsequent de colonization as in nationalism, then communism and now market socialism is a way to return back to its top rank that Chinese feel truly belong to them. To understand China, it might be a good idea to keep this

---

[1]Gordon Kerr. A Short History of China - From Ancient Dynasties to Economic Powerhouse. Pocket Essentials. Great Britain. 2013. Pg 38.

irrationality of the Chinese mind in reckoning that tries to overcome its state of underdevelopment and return to its historical glory.[2]

A return to the position of power in the Han, Tang and Song and later Qing dynasties those which have ruled over China in various ancient, medieval and modern times today secretly guides China's economic, social and military policies. One can never understand the inspired frenzy of the Chinese to produce the economic miracle which it has done until and unless one reckons this secret script of the Chinese mind to be able to retain its status as shaping the civilization of the world and the human race. The Chinese mind set is one in which the collective gets precedence over the individual and the desire to collectively achieve goals for an entire society has dominated the Chinese mind set in their great leap forward into the economic miracle. China has always been the leader of the global economy and its present political leadership has behaved from this high ground of historical memory.

Chinese Time is absolute and unchanging and there is a fixed image of things; everyday life obscures that image and it is the bounden duty of every individual and especially the heads of State to rediscover and reveal that image. Interestingly, the so-called economic miracle is also a search of this unchanging pattern of time immemorial. Paradoxically, Communism was also a strategy to seek out this permanent and indelible pattern; it was in no way any different in its intent as the reforms are and Mao and Deng are not as

---

[2]Lee Kuan Yew. The Grand Master's Insights on China, the United States and the World. Belfer Centre Studies in Internaional Security. USA. 2012. Pg8

opposites of one another as they seem; nor are Deng's reforms as drastically different from the policies pursued by Mao as they are made out to be. And both together tried to imitate some Han or Song emperor of the past[3].

As this manuscript is being finalized, China's trade surplus with the rest of the world has grown four times despite the severe recession sweeping its major export destinations the US and EU. China's exports seem to grow and grow and these are not merely cheap seconds and poor imitations of Japanese brands. China's exports today consist of arms, nuclear power equipment, sophisticated mining and transport machinery. China is steadily taking lead in agricultural exports as well beating the US and EU hollow. China appears to dominate not only the realm of consumer durables but also technology and capital goods. China's trade surplus is used to finance Chinese speculation in the world's natural resources; truly Chinese demand for iron ore, oil, and other minerals has sent the rest of us in a tizzy with mineral prices touching all time peaks and vis-à-vis China everyone else despairing to emerge as mineral exporters[4]! It is the same model that the colonized world has fallen into vis-à-vis England in the 19th and the 20th centuries. It appears as if China, in a similar pattern of trade and investments, is doing unto the world at large as the colonial powers had once done to make ancient civilizations under developed.

---

[3]General Tao Hanzhang's commentaries on Sun Tzu. The Art of War. The Book of Lord Shang, "Shang Yang". Wordsworth Classics of World Literature. Great Britain. 1987.

[4]Dambisa Moyo. Winner Takes All - China's Race For Resources and What It Means For All Of Us. Penguin. Great Britain. 2007. Pp7-9

China is not all consensuses for the country had fierce rebellions rioting and killing people, overthrowing and assassinating kings. Interestingly while rebels have tried to depose kings, they have also tried to unravel the real China and redeem its "real destiny". Rebels have been more like the tributaries of the great rivers of the land bringing with their conquests their cultures and wisdom and their desire to become a part of the great Chinese civilization. The main driving force behind China has been to recover its position as a world leader in civilization, something that China has always been. The Chinese policies of economic growth, military might and territorial identity have revealed the historical desire of the Chinese people to return to its days of glory under the Tang, Song, Ming and the Qing. The Chinese miracle is therefore much beyond a mere set of right economics; it is also the awakening into consciousness latent and dormant forces of civilization. To the best of my mind, it is the civilization aspect of the Chinese economic miracle which is more intriguing than discussing a set of economic policies. This book asserts that the Chinese economic miracle is only a return to its historical position which for a brief while was interrupted by the Western colonialism.

References:

1. Francis Fukayama. The Origins of Political Order – From Prehuman Times to the French Revolution. Profile Books. Great Britain. 2011

2. John Keay. China – A History. Harper Press. United Kingdom. 2008.

3. Paul Ropp. China In World History. OUP. Oxford. 2011.

4. Jonathan Mirsky. The Britannica Guide to Modern China. London. 2008.

Chapter Two

China's World View

The single question that underlies the quest in the present book is how did China grow so fast? One of the possible replies to this question lies in the nature of the Chinese ideology which entrenches a deep sense of agency among the people making the Chinese man at the centre of the Universe, in charge of his own life and commanding his own destiny. Interestingly, ancient Chinese ideology echoes the Protestant Ethics in medieval Europe where the idea of "being chosen" inspired entrepreneurship. Under this idea of "being chosen", entrepreneurs would actually make efforts to be successful so that people would think them to be especially blessed by God. For the Chinese too, material prosperity is virtue; unlike in India where poverty has been traditionally a virtue and riches have been equated with sin and corruption. There are two facts about China that strikes an amateur Sinologist; one is the appearance of the State and a Centralized government so early in human civilization in China and the other is the continuation of the Communist rule even after China being one of the most economically liberalized and globalized state in the world with perhaps the world's highest concentration of foreign investors. The present book suggests that both are connected to the Chinese world view.

Apart from the mere fact of economic growth, what also surprises the mind is that how the Chinese can rise together in a homogenous wave to the command of the Party Chairman just like a band of orchestra playing to the conductor's wand. A few historians like Paul Ropp[5] and John Keay[6] mention the amazing abilities of the Chinese to mobilize manpower for major projects like irrigation, dams and other infrastructure like roads and so on. Such mobilization has often happened through forced labour of conquered people and captured slaves[7]. These have been more for public works. But in most cases of organizing production, especially farming and food production, family based labour the Chinese have been quick to respond to commands emanating from the State. This rising to a call is not because the Chinese worker is passive and docile; nor is it because the Chinese is an unthinking, unreflective race, for China has known violent rebellions those which have challenged Emperors and fought conquerors. The Chinese is materialistic, loves material success, good builders of roads and dams, keen inventors and innovators and pragmatic in the use of science and technology. The collective mind of the Chinese derives straight out from the innate desire of being materially successful; self-interest of the people makes them cooperate with the fellow beings.

The Chinese do not seem to have much of a religion; neither the Prophetic ideology of the Semitic religions, nor

---

[5]Paul.S. Ropp. China in World History. OUP. NY. 2010. Pp 2-14.
[6]John Keay. China - A History. Harper. UK. 2008. Pg 27.
[7]Gordon Kerr. Op cit 1. Pp 20-21.

the speculative metaphysics of India. The Chinese believe in the power of Heaven, Heaven being the cosmos, inanimate and objective, moving out of inanimate physical laws. The Heaven works its way out through the rain, storm and thunder to arrive at equilibrium, and this equilibrium ensured a continued survival and indefatigability of the cosmos. Man is also a part of this world of objective reality, also subject to impersonal laws of the cosmos, he being a cog in the giant machinery. The prosperity of man depends upon his perfect alignment with the forces of nature. The action orientation of the Chinese thus is towards this alignment into the forces of the cosmos. In practical terms, this also means that the Chinese belief system has two aspects; one is to align one's action with the rest of the society and hence to play the game and the second is to emerge as a winner in that game. The Chinese society, because of its belief in the impersonal laws of the cosmos is eager to play in the herd so as not to be left out and to win in this competition. The Chinese are much into divination and astrology, only to discover 'what the Heaven has in mind'. Looked at in this way, the Emperor becomes one who spells out the rules of the game which every individual can thus play. In the language of Adam Smith, instead of the Invisible Hand of the market, Imperial decrees actually help coordinate and make meaningful numerous individual actions. Hence, the Emperor was something like the personification of the invisible forces; his decrees gave the much needed signals for the game that everyone would need to play. The willing submission of the people to empire and then to the highly centralized rule of the Communist Party and the commensurate unwillingness of the Chinese to enter into democracy vindicates the thesis that the Chinese must, in order to find meaning in life, act like a part of the Universe and then shine as its best[8].

Material prosperity in the Chinese system thus is a way of knowing that one has acted in accordance to the best interests of the Universe guided by impersonal laws. Emperors must show that they have the Mandate of Heaven; floods, famines, thunder and drought show that the rule of the emperor is not in alignment with the Mandate of Heaven[9]. Similarly personal wealth is a sign of being chosen, not unlike what Max Weber describes as the crux of Protestant Ethics. In his discussions on possible reasons why rational capitalism grew in England in the 18th century, Max Weber says that inter alia, the belief system of Protestant Christianity that said that God was unknowable and that rebirth was doubtful, one usually lived out Heaven and Hell upon this earth and being materially prosperous meant that one was chosen by God. Interestingly, a prosperous man in China was usually regarded as having acted in accordance to the principles of the cosmos and because of his correct alignment to its forces. Poverty was also then stupidity and had to be overcome. Poverty in China is neither valued as virtue as in Christian Europe, nor is it resigned to one's Fate as in India.

When we compare the Indian metaphysics along with the idea of transmigration of souls to Chinese fatalism, we observe interesting differences with China. In India, the human being

---

[8] I Ching - The Book of Changes. Various Internet sites.

[9] John Keay. Op cit 6. Pp53-55, 64-65 and various others.

is constituted by the cosmos; the cosmos ordains a certain fate for the human which constrains the limits of her actions. In China, the individual is also as inanimate as the Universe and both are guided by the same soulless rules and it is up to the individual, as an inanimate part of the Universe to fall in line with its rules. Metaphysics, philosophy and speculative spirituality are distant to the Chinese belief system and thought. Ideology for the Chinese is not so much a school of thought and a world view but a blueprint for action and roster for activity. The Chinese energy in bringing about economic prosperity must be seen in this light.

China has known the State system very early in the life of civilizations. In a way one could have only expected this. If the people are willing to work as forces of a Universe, what other human institution can mimic a Universe except a State? China has always looked for a centre to harmonize the actions of the numerous individuals and a centralized state has helped in this endeavour. In a contrast with India, where people have looked for an overarching dharma working as rules of behaviour and where the political power must uphold this dharma as the enabling atmosphere where rules of behaviour are followed universally, it has been possible for decentralized systems to survive under the universality of a social order. In China, politics has dominated the society, politics has made society viable; in India, and the state has been subservient to the society until after Independence. Such a feature in China helps explain why the Communist Party is as much as a social system as it is a political one.

The Imperial authority in China has to be benevolent

otherwise it is not seen to have the Mandate of Heaven. Oppressive regimes thus were overthrown with much rebellious confidence. The Chinese legends have three model Emperors who have kind and generous and this mythical Trinity forms the ideal type for the Chinese. Emperors deviating from this model have been deposed through peasant uprisings; Emperors, who followed this model, have armies of peasants defending them. No wonder then China has faced long periods of stability especially under the Song dynasty where rebellions seem to have disappeared and despite the vigil of wild tribes all around the Empire there have been no incursions. Empire in China is a social need; it is born out of the Chinese idea of the Universe, of its idea of human action, its desire for prosperity. Somehow this set of beliefs have not changed in China despite its swing from one extreme of moralist Confucianism and the other extreme of morally indifferent Legalism, from pragmatic Buddhism to fatalistic Daoism. It will not be very wrong to say that the Chinese history has a running theme sewing together many centuries of strife and success into a fair continuity.

As for the ideal common man, the Chinese extol the image of the farmer; he is the source of all work, of creativity, of innovation. He is the image of perfection, whose perfectness is the aim of the Emperor and all political authority that draws from it. This farmer is actually God, who with his wife and two children till the soil, grow crops and when he has grown enough for all to eat gets together other men and families to build canals, roads, homes. It is difficult to appreciate the centrality of the peasant in China until and unless one can appreciate the fact that the image of God in China is the peasant. The peasant produces food but not for the market; it is to be able to use the surplus to procure the services of more human beings to build infrastructure projects. The Emperor too is only an enlarged version of this ideal man in China and he moves human beings in want of food towards people who have produced surpluses so that hungry men and women find food and work[10]. This possibly explains why China has always been successful in moving millions from one place to another mobilizing through such movements, armies of workforce.

What we marvel in China today namely the ability of its people to rise in unison to centrally set targets, to value Communist rule despite the play of markets, the obedience and surrender to a cause and to maintain the political integrity of the state despite sweeping rebellions in the Tiananmen and all of this together to make for the astounding economic progress seems to have been genetically coded in the Chinese history. In the light of the above, the fact that China ever was poor, that China ever fell behind seems to be more of an anomaly than the fact that the country rose to keep over half of the world's production of goods and metals under its command.

The emphasis of the present book lies obviously in the economic reforms initiated in the era of Deng Xiaoping as Chairman of the Chinese Communist Party, hereafter referred to as the CCP. What comes under scanner is how Deng operated the freedom of the market under the centralized

---

[10]John Keay. Ibid. pp 26-27.

authority of the CCP. Deng promoted four modernizations; agriculture, industry, science and technology and military. Looked at from the perspective of Chinese history, Deng was only playing upon those forces that came together to produce economic miracles under the Sui and Tang period, or the Song and the Yuan ages. Deng is supposed to have reversed Mao's tenets of Communism but looked at closely we observe that Mao and Deng were not as different as the results of their policies were. Mao too tried to invoke the deeper principles of the Chinese people and especially the Cultural Revolution tried to relive the days of the Han Empire when the Chinese Emperor assumed the title of being the Cultural head of the society as also being its military head. Culture has been as important as unifying factor in China as military conquest and warfare has been. Along with market, culture and warfare have been unifying forces in China. Whether it is Mao or Deng, or Chiang Kai Sheik everyone has tried to establish the alignment of war, culture and market.

This book tries to emphasize the present economic miracle of China is located in the depths of its history and sociology, evolved through its politics than something which is only an outcome of macroeconomic policies. This means that the Chinese story cannot be replicated elsewhere in the world by repeating a set of impersonal and mechanical economics; instead the principles of its economic boom must be seen as a peculiar civilizational development of its society over time.

Empire and the CCP: Continuity in History

Though the state in China appeared very early in its history, social institutions of the family, the kingroups and tribes have been important as well. Localism, as in regional ties of tribalism and the centralized state has been in a constant strife. All through the Chinese history, regional kingdoms have tried to strike freedom from a central state and as soon as a regional power became powerful it tried to swallow its contemporaries into a centralized administration. Those empires have lasted long which have been able to negotiate these opposing trends of localism and centralism delicately and diplomatically. But there is nothing to suggest that centralism has served China better than localism for more infrastructure projects like dams, canals, roads and bridges have been constructed during regional states periods than under large centralized empires. Indeed, Chinese intellectual growth and the progress in science and technology appears to have done better during the Warring States period of 476 to 221 BCE, when Confucianism and Taoism were born and China graduated from the bronze to the iron age[11]. Intellectuals also proliferated during the Jin period between 265 and 420 CE, known as the age of war and death. Yet another fragmented Empire of the Sui Dynasty somewhat localised in the northern provinces of China did very well in the 6th and 7th CE in terms of building up the grand canal, a riverine route for trade and introduced the equal field system with corvee labour. The Tang Dynasty also fighting disunity introduced the printing

---

[11]Gordon Kerr. op cit 1. Pp 28-31.

press during the 9th and the 10th CE[12].

Apart from localism and centralism, China also had a second source of conflict in its society and which was between the Emperor and the Trader. The emperors came from the military and the military drew from the peasants; the trader was a different class altogether, sometimes an enemy of the peasant and therefore of the military, an extension of the peasant class and to the Empire. The advent of foreign trade of the Chinese has been through the management of the barbarians beyond its civilization in the form of the Huns, Manchus, Mongols and various other smaller tribes. Indeed, the Silk Road was first started by the Han Dynasty in the 2nd BCE to co-opt the Hun raiders who were looting the Chinese and merrily selling away stuff all the way to the Roman Empire through a relay system that included an understanding with many other tribes of Central Asia and Eastern Europe including the Khitans and the Kushanas and the Sakas. The trader then emerged as the powerful negotiator between China and the barbarians, sent out upon the vast tracts of what is now known as the Silk Road to reign in the barbaric forces and contain them by luring them into trade[13]. Traders have often become powerful, powerful enough to finance rebellions and blackmail regimes; they have been known to reorganize fields and production systems in order to extract their surpluses which have deprived the state of its revenues. Sometimes emperors have used the trader to collect taxes, allowing them to keep a part of it, invest it and retain

---

[12]Ibid. Various pages.
[13]Ibid. Pp 128-134.

the profits and after sometime make it over to the ruler. Such a system exists till today, where tax collectors and revenue officers intercept revenues going to the state, retains the same, and invests the same before handing it over to the ruler. In our day and age we call this as corruption; in China this has been a traditional tactic to incentivize the trader to fall in line[14].

In order to understand the rather strange phenomenon as spelled out above, one needs to understand the fundamental principles of economic organization in the country. The Chinese society throughout history has been primarily tribal and farming has been the main occupation. Whenever, the farmer has produced some surplus food, he has offered the same to other people and families and obtained, in exchange their labour. With this labour, the Chinese have levelled lands, built homes, extended fields and others. The keenness for the Chinese to develop infrastructure is endemic to the culture. Extrapolating this argument one may say that once the local population is exhausted, the Chinese would naturally look towards other outer societies to replicate similar models of economic activities and hence the conquests to expand territories of operation. The Shang Dynasty in 1600 BCE conquered lands of agrarian people in order to establish the Empire. The Han emperors expanded into the Hun territory for trade and the later Han also expanded into Vietnam to access the sea route of trade to Rome[15].

The peasant, soldier, emperor line has more or less been straight, often also a way of procuring forced labour and

---

[14]Paul. S. Ropp. op. cit 5. 2010. Pp 77-78.
[15]Gordon Kerr, Op cit 1.

slaves to work that field, grow that surplus by which larger communities can survive. Lui Ban, the founder of the Han Empire, China's utopia was a peasant. No example is better than the grand reaching out to tribes in the Three Kingdom Period of 220 – 340 CE in which peasants were whisked away by powerful landlords and prevented to produce goods for the empires. These were also times of flood, famine and pestilence. Natural calamities have wreaked havoc in China as have floods and the demand for war has risen proportionately during these times[16]. War has often been an instrument for annexing newer territories with newer people to trade with. Wars have been used to open up paths and roads to create passages of trade; indeed the Silk Road was seared through in order to rein in the wild Huns and the Khitans and through trade, co-opt these tribes into obeisance with the Chinese system. The Chinese used trade as much as war to expand their economic influence over the world. Given the present arms build-up in China, one can easily find that this is an age old formula of the Chinese to use profits first for self-consumption and then once satiated to use the same to engage in war. China, for the Chinese represents the world; territories that lie beyond it must be brought into the Chinese pale. This is why, for China, the limit is the entire world. This ideology gives China a wonderful opportunity for a trade and war economy.

The Chinese may have historically desired material prosperity rather than political freedom. The idea of individual freedom seems to be rather vague among the Chinese; the individual seeks importance as a social being, he

---

[16]John Man. The Great Wall. Bantam Books. Great Britain. 2008. Pg 73.

loves to command social respect and power but in a manner of the unattached, autonomous individual exercising his agency or his intellect was not among the top priorities of the Chinese culture. This possibly explains why economic growth eventually did not need the political freedom of democracy in modern day China. There have been conflicts of regionalism and centralism; provinces have often declared independence or cessation from the central Empire as in the case of the later Zhou, or the warring states period but rebellions have happened more out of economic considerations rather than for desires for political autonomy or cultural sovereignty.

Chinese people have also been active migrants. Hordes of Chinese have moved into islands in the South China Sea, filled up Japan, Korea, Vietnam, Myanmar and the islands of south East Asia. They have migrated as far as Turkey, overran central Asia and forayed into Siberia. The Chinese appear to be one of the world's largest spread of humanity. In the Chinese families there are stories of origin, families claim as their ancestral home, and places far beyond what they seem to ever have seen. Such stories imply that there has been rampant migration of population. Not only have traders migrated, but ordinary mortals have moved in droves, especially during famines when village after village moved out of their moorings in search of food for work in distant lands. Search for work and food have spurned large scale movement of people from one place to another. Interestingly, migrants have always searched cultural continuities for their comfort in new territories. The idea of a Chinese Empire emanated also as spatial Universe for cultural continuities for the migrants. It is small wonder then that migration forms a major legitimising force for a large Chinese empire[17].

China, like India has a long and continuous history for nearly five millennia and yet there is little consciousness of change. In the Chinese imagination the world has gone on in the same rhythm ever since hoary memories punctured temporarily by storms and floods, rain and snow and rebellions, overthrows, conquest and consolidation. China can be understood China's self-image is the role of its society as the epitome of human civilization, repository of its morals, and the peak of its intellect. It is this self-image that China is seeking to establish all over again. A possible reason for the continuity of the Chinese history may in fact have been its poor political culture and a strong social culture, something that seems to brace China even to this day. A poor political culture means that the inner contradictions of the Chinese society in terms of regionalism versus localism, the family versus the larger society, private morals versus civic sense, social prestige versus engagement in work, trader versus the emperor, peasant versus the trader, north west hilly and arid region and the south eastern flat deltaic zone somehow remains in force even to this day. However, a strong social culture means that these have been fairly absorbed and tolerated and made space for within the system of social reproduction in which these contradictions attain equilibrium,

---

[17]In Martin Jacques. When China Rules the World - The End of The Western World and the Birth of a New Global Order. Penguin. 2nd Edition. Great Britain. 2012. Pg 98. "These (clan groups) were huge extended kinship groups, which traced their origins back to a common male ancestor."

though uneasy[18].

References:

1. Francis Fukayama. The Origins of Political Order – From Prehuman Times to The French Revolution. Profile Books. Great Britain. 2011.

2. John Keay. China – A History. Harper Press. United Kingdom. 2008.

3. Paul Ropp. China In World History. OUP. Oxford. 2011.

---

[18]Ibid.

Chapter Three

Ancient Chinese Economy and Polity

China's ancient economic production structure contained exactly the very same social, political and economic forces as prevail in the country today. Perhaps one of the reasons why China is regarded as an ancient civilization is because forces that shaped its society and the productive forces remain ever much the same with an unbroken continuity since time immemorial[19].

In the hoary days of Chinese history we see that the level of attainments of its productive forces had developed faster than anywhere else in the world. For instance, the level of agricultural and industrial that China attained in 10,000 BC where of advanced Neolithic vintage when the world was still in its Mesolithic stage. The Chinese civilization could manage to develop very well because of the discovery of Neolithic tools that helped agriculture as well as metallurgy. It seems that metallurgy helped the Chinese make tools and therefore to extend cultivation[20].

---

[19]"A special feature of Chinese civilization is that it seems to have no beginning. It appears in history less as a conventional nation-state than a permanent natural phenomenon." In Henry Kissinger. On China. Penguin. USA. 2012. Pg 5.

[20]Jian Bozan, Shao Xunzheng and Hu Hua. A Concise History of China. Foreign Languages Institute. Beijing.PPR China. 2nd edition. 1984. Pp 5-10.

As early as the during this stage, the Chinese ruling class which formed some kind of empire by use of force and war had bronze and silk factories in which large scale labour would work with big collective farms that employed farmers as labourers in order to supply food for the industrial workers. Unlike in the West, where manufactures seemed to have developed out of the agrarian surpluses, in China, farming appears to have been planned keeping in mind the needs of labour in the manufacturing sector. Our pedagogy is far too used to treating small farming societies as a universal trend in history because of evidence from anthropological surveys of primitive and small human societies and also because of European societies having been basically peasant societies, we tend to regard small farming societies as being the rule of evolution. China may have been and most probably have been different and though the dream of the Chinese man is to be a farmer with a wife and child, cultivating his own food, this dream possibly was there because the objective conditions did not guarantee his home, hearth and haven. China may have been suited more to collective farming than individual farming and when eventually the individual farming became permitted by the State and especially legalised as a legitimate way of growing food, canals had been dug, flood plains created, water sheds erected and dikes built. The need for infrastructure as would allow the Chinese to emerge out of the collective into the individual may as well have been the prime moving force of the Chinese history. Indeed, the Chinese seem to have led their soldiers into the farming communities in order to be able to integrate and absorb the food producing societies within their own[21].

Historically China has emerged out of adventuring soldiers, who could gather men, grab swathes of land, access trade routes deploying some men as workers in manufacture, some as peasants in collective farms and some as soldiers to fight and loot. This is somewhat the way Shang, often known as the first Empire, somewhere between 1600 to 1045 BCE came to rule. The Shang Empire was less of an empire held together by some kind of governance; in fact, the Shang was like a large private property with royal fields for crops and grazing land for animals. The Shang system was very close to the slave system and expectedly the ancient Chinese people under the ancient Shang were oppressed by royal forces, often buried alive as slaves with the corpses of kings and had little personal freedom. It seems that the royal factories were also prisons for the ordinary people. This system changed with the coming of the Zhou dynasty which ruled China between 1045 and 771 BCE[22].

The Shang forayed into lands beyond the vicinity and appropriated them. The workers in these lands were turned into corvee labour. The peasant doubled up as the factory worker and the soldier. Soon peasants sliced off some of the imperial power, gathered arms, conquered lands and settled as mini Shangs in the outlying regions of the Shang kingdom. The force of independent peasants, who were also armed, made it difficult for the Shang to retain hold as the sole

---

[21]Ibid. There is evidence of large scale and organized slavery in ancient China.

[22]Gordon Kerr. Op cit. 1.

economic agent. The rise of the independent peasant who now could think of becoming his own dream man with a wife by his side and a child a top his shoulder and a field of his own was made possible because of the vast progress made during the Shang in terms of technology and irrigation. The technological advances of the Shang empowered a people into peasantry and a slew of independent peasant became the backbone of the succeeding Zhou Empire[23].

The major difference between the Shang and the Zhou was that while the former was an extended private property, the latter was a source of governance and law, in which the Empire allowed people to work as independent households and groups on their own land and exchange products among them. The decline of the Shang and the rise of the Zhou were based on some interesting changes in circumstances which have braced the course of Chinese history repeatedly. The Zhou maintained the Shang achievements especially in technology. Some scholars feel that the Zhou signalled the rise of feudalism in China in which the empire connected with the subjects through a series of tribute paying intermediaries. It is not so certain that this was the case[24].

The foundation of the Zhou Empire was the independent peasant while the foundation of the Shang Empire was the private merchant. The latter subjugated people into slavery and forced labour but the former addressed the aspirations of the people to be free. The establishment of the nobility was a go between arrangement between the large private merchant

---

[23]Ibid
[24]Ibid Pp 11 to 20

and the independent peasant; it was more of a transition between the Shang polity and the final aspirations of the Zhou utopia. This makes the Zhou feudalism quite different from the European feudalism that emerged out of a particular manner of appropriating farm surpluses.

There are epigraphic evidences to show that land was also a traded commodity, also a way to consolidate lands into the hands of the powerful persons though royal land was disaggregated and distributed to individual members to enhance the generation of marketable surpluses. The changes in the economy and land ownership system under the Zhou were ways to help revenues from the subjects flow directly into the imperial coffers. Commerce, rather than a series of landed intermediaries helped channelize the revenues from households to the Empire. Apropos to this, commerce which started during the Shang were promoted under the Zhou and a new title "Jia' was invented for the merchant class to signify the importance of this category of economic agents[25].

The method of using commerce to collect revenues stirred up the economy and soon there emerged wealthy individuals with wide economic and social networks. These zones of economic prosperity along with growing social networks created people who now looked towards becoming kings and even Emperors themselves. This led to a series of assertions and political competition between contenders of power and made this period be known to history as the Warring States Period. There must have been wars, but this was also a period of great construction. River dams, roads, canals, temples were

---

[25]John Keay. China - A History. op cit 6

built and large public works undertaken. The merchant class that rose to great importance during the Zhou period doubling up also as a revenue channelling agent was sought to be replaced by a more open system via a dedicated bureaucracy. The merchants were people with contacts among the nobility and imperial family while the bureaucracy that was being set up in the warring states was open to one and all and recruitment was through a written examination. The Warring States raised an impersonal and open bureaucracy[26].

Incessant competitive wars appear to have ended in 221 BCE as the smaller states consolidated under the Qin dynasty. The Qin system was a throwback to the Shang era where the Emperor was cruel and the system would run on strict legalistic principles. People were banned from keeping arms and a Mao Zedong like system of meeting production target emerged. The Qin dynasty was overthrown in 206 BCE but it unified China and set out is boundaries in such a manner that China derives its name from Qin. The unpopular Qin was replaced by the Han, a de ja vu of the imperial Zhou overthrowing the Shang dynasty.

If the Qin dynasty had given China its present territory, it was the Han dynasty which set up the values and morals of China as a civilization. Under the Han, the golden mean was achieved between a strong centralized government and autonomous economic agents mainly the peasant. The local economies and the central government found its golden mean of sharing surpluses and mutually fulfilled each other. The moral foundation of China which seeks to find that

---

[26]Op cit 20. Pg 15 and John Keay op cit 25

perfect equilibrium between values and prosperity, respect and success, individual fulfilment and duties as a social being, the Heavenly forces and the Hellish fiends was more or less established during the Han period. The Han made it possible by moving its political machinery closer to align the extremes of the Shang and the Qin into acceptable compromises. The Han dynasty had strong state owned enterprises as also smaller enterprises, developed local and provincial councils, much like the ones in modern China, began the household registration systems to track able bodied individuals capable of rendering labour. Corvee was nearly abolished, cruel punishments based on eye for eye abolished and a system of justice based upon moral principles and jurisprudence developed. The Han period is China's Golden Age, referred in the most idyllic terms.

The history of China alternates between two extremes. One is a decentralized system with openness in administration, fairness and justice, morals and values and power to the individual cultivator and unifying the country with commerce. The other is an authoritarian state concentrating the forces of production in its hands, using forced labour and making military aggression as its raison d'etre. The latter kinds of governments were legalistic in nature, had little scope for justice and morality and were usually unpopular and faced violent rebellions. Commerce in the first case of egalitarian States was often a means of collecting revenues while in case of the latter, military aggression went along with revenue collection. Both trade as well as war was a means to raise levels of aggregate demand which in turn helped agricultural production and industrial enterprises grow.

The Han period was marked also by conflicts between the Confucianist scholars favouring laissez faire economy where the market would dominate while there were modernizers who believed in a strong centre with high taxation. Legalism, the principles that favoured a strong state and Confucianism that advocated social duties where everyone had its own space came into a conflict. The Hans were more inclined towards Confucianism. It is pertinent to note that the taxation had been greatly moderated to allow the economic agents function freely. With such liberal policies of the State, merchants who traded in salt and iron became very rich and started buying up land. Since iron and salt industry employed very large number of labourers, the people were inclined to be more loyal to these large industrialists than the State. The State in turn started nationalizing the salt and the iron industries to curb the powers of merchants. The major conflict during the Han period was between the merchants and the Emperor but the peasants continued to live in peace and prosper. The conflict between the trader and the peasant had a major outcome, the unified currency of the Qin regime was foregone, though the standard weights and measures remained[27].

Whether the Empire allowed laissez faire or opted for central command of the economy, there were always three reasons for the state owned enterprises in China. One was to curtail the powers of the merchants who would often become very powerful and command loyalties of soldiers and peasants; secondly, the State kept the manufacture of

---

[27]Gordon Kerr op cit 1. Pp 28-32.

military equipment and uniform to itself and hence needed enterprise to feed and clothe and equip the army. The third reason for the State to intervene in the economy was to be able to help with the public distribution of grain and other items of everyday necessity which if fallen to market forces might lead to speculation and price rise. Famines in China were dangerous for political regimes and they were not rare.

In fact irrespective of the kind of State which China had trade and war were the two instruments with which the surpluses produced in its fields and factories could be focussed towards the State; if such surpluses were to circulate around in the society, rich merchants would use these to buy up land and consolidate power and then rebel against the State. Trade and war thus went hand in hand to protect Empires. It was not until the Sui (581 to 618 CE) and then the Tang (618 to 907 CE) dynasty that the sale of land was prohibited.

Since land seemed to be the currency of trade and investments, credit would be advanced against land and land would be sold to settle debts, rich merchants obtained land and then employed labour into such lands. Landowners became prospective contenders of political power and often raised armies. Thus iron merchants, salt traders, silk manufacturers often accumulated land, employed labour, got the latter's loyalties and raised armies to attack kingdoms and empires. The Sui dynasty and then the Tang banned the sale of land to stall the possibilities of such accumulation of assets that often helped raise rebellions. Currency was introduced as paper money because money was assured rather than actually transacted. It must be recalled that commerce had an intricate connection with state revenues especially in regimes which allowed the peasants to retain their own land and surpluses produced out of that land. The revenues on land or on enterprises was transferred all the way to the capital through a series of commercial transactions and for this paper money served as a useful medium. However, paper money was backed by bronze[28].

Once the sale of land was banned, employment of labour on land became a political issue; questions like whether labour will own land and the surplus; or will own land but not the surplus; or will have neither land nor surplus are issues over which leaders as late as Mao Zedong and Deng Xiaoping have debated. Most political changes in China took place around the issue of land and labour which finally culminated in Communism under Mao in 1949. The system of leasing out land, fixing production targets for peasants, organizing of teams, rewarding the productive and punishing the lazy has intertwined China's politics and economics, state and society, the administrator and the economic agent as nowhere else in the world. Also, after the delegalizing the sale of land, a peculiar system of land grants begin in which emerges a nobility created by the State; perhaps the real beginning of feudalism which never quite grows roots under the Chinese system because decentralized power hardly ever stabilizes in the intermediaries.

If we are to identify the basic units for the study of the Chinese economy we observe the following. There

---

[28] Paul S. Ropp. Op cit 5, China in History

is a peasant family producing food on a patch of land, there are groups of families who exchange the surplus food among themselves mainly to procure labour power, labour power is used for construction of private homestead and also infrastructure like building roads, digging canals and levelling land (interestingly such peasant groups invest labour power in building infrastructure and it is not merely a royal affair), trade routes are important for the collective surplus to travel out and earn surpluses to accumulate more land and hence more labour. This is roughly the image of China under a laissez faire economy. States attempt to control the economy when merchants become too strong and impose various bans; the main ban being on independent trade and State monopolises trade and carries it out through the members of the royal family or a closed network of trusted nobility. Sometimes, State does not wish to intervene in the laissez faire and instead wages warfare to create a demand for goods and services and thereby inviting the loyalties of the people again. Sometimes, empires are peaceful; they do not wish to wage wars, nor are they too keen to takeover businesses for revenues. In these cases, the governments set up elaborate systems of household registration systems, decentralized units of government and actively promote trade so that surpluses from the ground propel towards the empire through this route. Imperial tax collectors procure revenues from a series of traders below who exchange goods and keep profits for themselves and even speculate on revenues before handing them into the Imperial coffers. What we define as corruption in China because government officials are always trading and speculating before passing on the revenues to the State is actually an age old convention developed out of the Chinese needs[29].

References:

1. Francis Fukayama. The Origins of Political Order – From Prehuman Times to The French Revolution. Profile Books. Great Britain. 2011.

2. John Keay. China – A History. Harper Press. United Kingdom. 2008.

3. Paul Ropp. China In World History. OUP. Oxford. 2011.

4. William.A.Joseph. Politics in China – An Introduction. OUP. USA. 2010.

---

[29] Ibid

Chapter Four

The Opium War

The significance of the Opium War cannot be understood until and unless one understands the foundations of the Qing Dynasty, the last of China's imperial rulers after which one finds the advent of Nationalist and eventually of Communist China. The Qings were the Manchu people in the north western border of China who evicted the Mongol kings by the name of Ming which ruled China over three centuries between the 14th and the 17th. The Manchus adopted symbols of water and azure for their Empire as opposed to the symbols of fire of the Ming who they overthrew. In the language of the I Ching, and the "Mandate of Heaven" it was the defeat of the fire by water and hence promised a more adaptive, quieter, peaceful, prosperous rule than the warring Ming. The Ming dynasty seemed to have risen on the unity of the Mongol tribes and it fell similarly upon their disunity. The internecine tribal war was waged on competition among groups in order to gain larger shares of the commerce raked up by the activities on the Silk Road. During the Ming regime, the government insisted on collecting taxes in silver which meant that households were forced to sell their produce in the market against a price. The age old system of China's mutual interdependence among peasant households and the barter system of trade began to be changed; now one needed money in order to be able to pay taxes. This created fissures in the Chinese society in which the tribal unity among the Ming's was broken. The insistence on a standard exchange system or currency has been always fraught with trouble in China and during the Ming times, this issue raked up again. However, the onset of a mini Ice Age in 1626 also caused famines, rebellions, conflicts[30].

Demands of money and the bulk and weight of metallic money together with the fear of robbers along the trade routes developed the institution of banking in China in which banks gave paper bonds against deposits and issued credit notes against credit. The banking system brought forth the Buddhists and the Wing people are supposed to have drawn inspiration from Bodhisattva Manjusri. In fact, all the while in the Ming rule there were rebellions against the Mongols in the form of White Lotus groups and other secret societies which plotted the fall of the Machus[31]. The rise of the Qing was the re ushering of the Buddhist dominated Confucianist ethics of laissez faire economy.

The Qing consolidated the empire not by fighting but by building bridges with the Mongols on the one hand and the Han people on the other. They continued with the Ming policy of collecting taxes in money and invoked pretty much the similar chain of merchants who exchanged money, issued debt papers and made deposits in banks. But

---

[30]Ibid.

[31]Jonh Man, The Mongol Empire - Genghis Khan, His Heirs and The Founding of Modern China. Bantam Press. UK. 2014. Pg 288.

the Qing era saw two major developments over the Ming era; commerce naturally grew manifold under the Qing as did various kinds of industries but there also emerged a certain level of unemployment because the internal synergy which was the typical Han way of life among the peasant households was broken under the pressure of having to earn more money through the sale of one's surpluses rather than circulate the same among the society for mutual economic cooperation. Production of silk, manufactured items, luxury goods and even food increased as did commerce and silver rang into the Imperial coffers. The Qing, a Taoist dynasty, seeking cultural refinement and pursuing literature and poetry nonetheless took up arms against the Russians in Tibet and Taiwan and arbitrarily attacked Korea; warfare being a means of generating employment. The Qing period saw the Chinese economy grow but lose the internal synergy that China was used to. Also during the Qing, the power of the Mandarins really grew; they wore long sleeves, grew nails to show that they did not need to work. There was contempt for manual work and for all those who did so; this was a kind of colonialism and indeed, in the Chinese mind, it was not the period of the Western powers but the Ming and the Qing that started the enslavement of China.

The Mandarins morally corrupted China by being bad role models. For the Chinese, it is very important to imitate the powerful and successful citizens and now under the Qing they imitated the Mandarins. Mandarins were lazy, narcissists, exploitative and averse to work; soon the Chinese started emulating these loathsome attributes. The Chinese addiction to Opium was to a large extent a fashion of the Mandarins[32].

The Opium war was waged because while the Europeans especially the British demanded all kinds of Chinese goods including jade, tea, metals, spices, herbs, porcelain and others, with tea topping the list, China did not seem to want anything from Europe or Britain. Since the payments for Chinese foreign trade had to be made with silver, Britain lost a lot of silver to China. Therefore, Britain had to look for a particular commodity which could be exported to China in order to get the silver back and continue buying the Chinese products. Opium was exported to China from India in such large quantities that the silver flowed back from China into Britain's East India Company and ravaged China through opium addiction. When the Chinese Emperor took steps against Britain, the first Opium War broke out in which Britain defeated the Qing Emperor. China was humiliated and was forced to sign the Treaty of Nanjing in which China had to pay for waging the war and also concede Hong Kong to Britain[33].

The question remains as to why did the Chinese demand opium so much? To the Chinese mind, opium had many medicinal properties as well as aphrodisiac value. It was largely believed in China that opium helped one beget male children; male preference being a perpetual scourge in the Chinese society. Besides, one must never lose sight of the fact that medicine was one of the largest imports of China from all over the world, especially India. The Indian medicines

---

[32]Julia Lovell. The Opium War - Drugs, Dreams and the Making of China. UK. 2011. Pp 17 to 22
[33]Ibid.

were valued in China and medicines from Assam, Manipur and Kashmir made brisk business. Opium was supposed to increase immunity, fight disease and ensure good health. It was a medicine which was associated also with material prosperity and high fashion because of the Mandarin culture. Expectedly then, when during the Qing, consumerism and ostentation was at its height in China, demand for opium, the elixir of life also increased[34].

The colonization of China was complete after the Second Opium War in which the powers Britain, France, United States of America and Russia joined in to parcel China into their own territories. The Opium Wars lay the foundation of the loot of China by the Western powers as well as Japan. While the relationship between the Western powers and China changed with the WWII when the erstwhile colonisers invested heavily in the outlying territories of China, namely Taiwan and Hong Kong trying to keep their shipping industries and control over sea trade routes alive, Japan continued to occupy Manchuria for excavating China's minerals.

[34]Op cit. 5

References:

1. China's Opium War.   Frank Dikotter.(incomplete reference)

2. US Country Studies.http://lcweb2.loc.gov/frd/cs/cntoc.html

3. Economic History of China Before 1912. Wikipedia. Internet Sources.

Chapter Five

Resurrection of China

It is only expected that a proud people such as the Chinese would never have taken the humiliation in the hands of the foreigners with any equanimity. Rebellions against the incumbent Qing dynasty tore across China starting with the famous Taipeing Rebellion between 1850 and 1864 which killed anywhere between 20 to 30 million people in civil war. The rebellion was directed at the Qing Dynasty and because the foreign powers helped the Emperor crush the rebellion down mercilessly, rebels resolved more strongly to eradicate the Qing and everything that the Qing stood for including China's prosperity. Taipeing Rebellion was as obscure as it was modern; its founder being a Han Chinese, Hong Xiuquan who failed the civil services and became a cynic towards the Qing Dynasty. He gathered a small force in the Guanxi province and then spread elsewhere in China especially in the south and South West demanding that Chinese should modernize and Christianize. Hong claimed him to be the younger brother of Jesus Christ and demanded a series of reforms in the Chinese society which was to abolish the various restrictions on women, do away with gender based social differentiation and socialize land ownership. Hong said that all religions and faiths intrinsic to China should be abolished and only Christianity must be adopted. The Christian Western powers were shocked at Hong's claims and helped Qing in crushing the rebellion but Taiping had very strong appeal for both nationalists and the Communists in the 20th century China.

The Taiping Rebellion also asserted an ethnic Chinese identity against the Manchu identity of the Qing. The Qing dynasty had a dualistic policy; one was to show tolerance towards the society at large but the other was to insist that men shave their heads and wear pigtails in the manner of the Manchus if they wished to be favoured by the State. Since the Han Chinese believed that the hair on the head belongs to one's ancestors and ancestors are the sacred ones in a society which does not have a transcendental religion with Gods and Goddesses, dictates such as these were humiliating for the society in general. Hong cashed on this sentiment, wore hair loose and earned the epithet of being "hairy rebels". Despite its obscurities and fundamentalisms, the rebellion created a sense of Chinese pride, laid an agenda for obliterating the gender divide and called for socialism through collectivization of land. Both such strains worked well towards the creation of sentiments of modernity, socialism, nationalism and then Communism. Mao Zedong was especially moved by the Taiping Rebellion and admired its founder[35].

The Taiping Rebellion's understanding of the Chinese catastrophe at the Opium Wars was as follows. The Chinese lost out to the Western powers because they were not prepared

---

[35]Immanuel C.Y. Hsu. The Rise of Modern China. Sixth Edition. OUP. USA. 2000. Pp 220-255

militarily to fight the West. They were not prepared because they did not modernize their arms and ammunitions; they did not modernize because they were distracted with useless money making pursuits by selling and consuming opium. They could find a vast market for opium only because they were driven by some obscure Chinese beliefs that opium could produce male heirs and prolong longevity. Agents who sold opium could do so only because China was overwhelmingly a market economy and had the means to buy anything and everything from an open market against silver; the pursuit of market destroyed its synergic village economy that often had the power to protect the people against famines and poverty. Eventually in the later day processes of decolonization, the Nationalists believed in the modernization of the army, acquiring state of art weapons and replacing Qing merchants with Han Chinese ones. The Communists believed that the village and its farming must be restored and modern industry which was at par with the Western powers be set up by using the food surpluses and rationalizing the deployment of the labour force among the various sectors, namely the military, agriculture, construction and industry.

The Taiping Rebellion stirred up many levels of rebellions in China all of which did not have clear goals to pursue. The Nian rebellion happened in the North and North West of China in response to a natural calamity namely the Yellow River flood in 1851[36]. However, there were some Muslim separatist movements such as the Dungan and the Panthay; and the intra Muslim ethnic clashes between the

---

[36]John Keay, op cit 6, pg 467

Punti and Hakka clans. There was also the Miao rebellion against the Han Chinese people. These rebellions presented the divisive elements within the Chinese society making both the Nationalists and Communists resort to agendas and programmes and even militarizations to contain such centrifugal forces. These divisive forces had land and arms and were related to the Chinese system in fractals rather than as organic wholes. Hence, China could never risk democracy for the fear of being torn asunder by groups that had localized visions of their history rather than an overall understanding of China in its territorial vastness and cultural plurality[37].

Unlike India, China was never wholly a colonized economy. Its economic organization since the Song dynasty in the 12th century has been quite continuous till the 20th century. The Chinese economy has been described as being "bottom heavy" where numerous independent peasant households would produce food and other cash crops and trade among themselves and often use surpluses in food to procure labour for various purposes such as land levelling, pond filling or deepening of water bodies. The Chinese markets are very well developed and lie deep into the interior. In fact this organization of production made it so easy for the East India Company to get the farmers to produce tea and buy opium as if in a unison. The existence of numerous producers who actively exchange goods among themselves with wide networks of trade makes China a land with very strong powers of acting upon market signals. Mao's Communism tried to repress this market power in order to force peasants work

---

[37] Ibid, pp 467- 478.

within the community and enter into relationships only with the State; Deng returned China to its innate principle of decentralized production.

The only thing which can genuinely misbalance China has been its population. In a system of neat exchanges spare population can only be used to extend cultivation into other lands or to fight wars. In case of China, wars have been a means of deploying excess labour which eventually have led to larger tracts of land getting cultivated in conquered lands. Such systems make China appear as a land which is constituted in a modular manner with distinct and different economic zones. Hence we observe that China is composed of macro regions where geography, culture, ethnicity and history are as different as the respective economies[38].

Since the Ming Dynasty in the 14th century, China has experienced an increase in population; the Chinese assigned this to a decline in deaths made possible by developments in medicine, many of which would come via the Silk Road from India and Tibet. The Chinese also believed that opium would help in producing male children, a cultural preference for the people there. This made the Chinese hanker for opium and produce tea in their farms. The productions of tea made the Chinese move away from the food crops and also pursue chains of commerce which had opium traders at the other end. Food for food was no longer exchanged; food for cotton was not exchanged and the synergy among the producers in the local economy was snapped in favour of the British traders who came via the various villages but from far away coasts of

---

[38]Ibid

the Pearl River Delta where the foreign agents including many Indians were anchored. The tea-opium trade created not only food scarcity but also snapped the internal cohesion of the Chinese systems of production. Yet another casualty was the textile industry where the smaller weavers and spinners lost out on the synergic supply of raw cotton and even labour.

In this background the Chinese were battling their hurt egos at China being so humiliated in the Opium Wars necessitated a programme of modernization which, in their eyes consisted of modern science, technology and industry. China's modernization started under the Qing dynasty and between 1860 and 1865 the state sponsored what is known as the Self Strengthening Movement for institutional reforms. Under this effort at modernization, China used foreign technology to build railways, ship yards and modernise the army[39]. Modern industries were set up in the coastal areas of the Pearl River Delta, an area where the foreigners especially Britain, France and United States were ensconced. Chinese were employed here; their engineers and scientists learnt much about modern technology and industry. The textile industry wiped out the indigenous handloom of China as did the modern silk industry. Indian and Ceylonese plantations were used to produce tea and the demand for Chinese tea also collapsed leaving China bereft of its main item of earning foreign exchange.

The incidence of foreign investments and the various war tribunals that made China pay for the Opium war increased debts. Meanwhile the Japanese, out of its strategy

---

[39]Op cit 5. Pp 282 to 287.

of procuring raw materials for its various industries especially the steel industry invested heavily in Manchuria, where most of China's natural resources are found. These areas are rich in deposits of iron ore, coal, tin, tungsten and uranium, all important for Japan's industries. The programme of modernization in the 1860's looked much like Deng's modernization a century later.

China historically had a preference for roads and connectivity and spared substantial efforts at creating infrastructure at the local levels. This network would support hectic trade, part cash, part barter where families and households actively exchanged goods and ware among themselves. But wars and rebellions destroyed this network and unless the roads were repaired the plan of rural development appeared jeopardised. Massive construction projects were undertaken which again needed labour from the countryside and also more food stocks to feed the workers. The Qing government was far too centralized to mobilise labour from deep inside the hinterland and moved towards focussing development on the south east tracts of China, separated by rugged mountains from the cold and arid lands of the North West and where the weather was hot and humid. A century later, Deng would rediscover the power of the delta to launch his modernizations from, a rather surprising similarity to the Qing modernization.

While China's pride was punctured with the foreign domination and the Chinese reasoned that it was their lack of modern amenities that eventually defeated them to foreign powers, yet they did not take to the modernizing drive with unalloyed enthusiasm; indeed there was more resistance to modernization than acceptance because the Chinese felt that machines would take jobs away and make manual labour redundant. Modernization was also accompanied by a rise of population which made it imperative to grow more food. Irrigation was extended and many new crops like the sweet potato and maize were cultivated. Yet, farm production decreased and food shortage loomed large. A possible reason for such economic catastrophe in the event of modernization was that expenses soared and it made more sense for men to seek work outside farms and for the women to stay back home with their cottage industries instead of taking up factory work. The textile industry, one of the leading industries of China before the Opium Wars took a beating from the home based cottage industries. The Chinese industries have often retreated; Mao used the might of the home based production to help the country grow under Communism; Deng used the path of the large industries located in the industrially advanced geography of the coastal areas.

China also suffered at the hands of a fellow Asian power namely the Japanese during the WWII. Unlike the Western powers, Japan did not involve the Chinese; Chinese were not employed in its units, the positions were all reserved for the Japanese people. Also Japan did not develop a network of Chinese units those could have served the Japanese industry. Instead, Japanese presence really disturbed the synergy in the Chinese manufacturing. The Japanese also created Machuko, a nearly autonomous zone in Manchuria. Though the trade between China and Japan helped China earn foreign exchange which it was otherwise losing to Britain and the United States, Japan's attitude towards China in treating it as a cesspool did not go down too well it is nationalism. China attacked Japan in which Britain and United States towed the line. This was in the year 1937 and by 1939 as the WWII broke out; Japan was on the other side of the allies. In fact, the Japanese atrocities committed on the Chinese were so severe that generations of Chinese still recall with horror what in history is known as the "Other Holocaust". The allies, namely America and Britain came into its aid and after the war was over invested heavily in Taiwan and Hong Kong in heavy industries needed for rebuilding the nation. China is a land that pursues military might and high ego. It was felt that the nationalists were too weak to be able to restore China into its old glory.

On the one hand there was a national humiliation and oppression by the Japanese and on the other hand there was an economic crisis brought more with modernization than out of the lack of it. There was arrogance of the Manchu officials and the inefficacy of the Qing State machinery to deliver material prosperity, there were numerous anti modernistic assertions as well. In other words, resistances of every kind soared to the incumbent Qing dynasty precipitating a change of order in China. From the mutual struggle among people, Sun Yat Sen's principles of modernization, democratization and sovereignty rose as the overarching theme for China. As has been the history of China troubled times seem to produce a surfeit of literary activists; the late 19th and the early 20th century saw the rise not only of litterateurs but also of literary societies that would play a significant role in organizing revolutionary movements throughout China. This age was the golden age of Chinese intelligentsia with free flowing public opinions, ideologies, arguments and discourses about politics, morality and the economy[40].

The Communists opposed the Nationalists in the sense it wanted every foreign power to leave China; China looked towards a grand isolation perhaps for the first time ever in its history. Communism doubled up here as nativism and isolationism. Japanese occupation of Manchuria had already cut China off from its historically vast economic base in south East Asia, a region which Japan occupied. In many ways, China was already isolated economically and politically. Communism was a way to regain the Chinese control over China. The nationalists too were in favour of full autonomy and political sovereignty but they could not take a full-fledged stance in favour of nativism because they felt that the western powers could give them the much needed technology for modernization. It is not as if that the Communists were anti-technology but they believed that technology could be endogenously produced from within the society if the people could produce enough surpluses to invest into personnel engaged into scientific endeavour; they also believed that the innate desire of humans to do well made them invent their necessities. The Nationalists were not so romantic or optimistic; they were in haste to drive out the colonisers and for which they needed arms and ammunition to wage wars. Modernization, the Nationalists felt would at least be needed, if not for the economy then at least for the military.

---

[40]Ibid.

The birth of Communism in China is not new. It hails from its long history of rebellions in which rebels gathered peasant forces, seized central power and then redefined the moral culture for the entire Empire. Communism gathered similar peasant forces, organized them into a party and used this peasant force for doing what the nationalists were doing with elite leadership. The Nationalists believed in the modernization of the army, acquiring state of art weapons and replacing Qing merchants with Han Chinese ones. The Communists believed that the village and its farming must be restored and modern industry which was at par with the Western powers be set up by using the food surpluses and rationalizing the deployment of the labour force among the various sectors, namely the military, agriculture, construction and industry[41].

There were two areas of crisis because of which the Communists gained predominance; one was the destruction of infrastructure due to the Sino Japanese war and the other was the reluctance of the foreign powers situated in what in modern times would look like a Special Economic Zone. While in the former one needed to rebuild the destroyed roads and canals, in the latter one needed more autonomy to be able to raise taxes and revenues in order to be able to pay for war. The Nationalist government took to printing notes in order to make the payments for the Sino Japanese War and this created hyperinflation on one hand and famines on the other. It was in this backdrop that the Communist took over powers in 1949 and started the political and economic reconstruction of the

[41]Jian Bozan et al. Concise History of China.

nation[42].

There were two sides to the Communist programme; one was to appropriate all systems of production, large and small from private players into the hands of the government and the other was to go for deep autarky in the face of isolation. The other was to allow peasants retain their autonomy and have decentralized systems of enforcing a more equitable distribution of goods. Mao's brand of Communism appeared to follow the former while the many rebels harped on the latter model of decentralized autonomy. In the Maoist programme, peasant lands were confiscated by the State and peasants were converted to workers in the land. The food produced in the arable lands was used to feed the industrial labourers into the city and the State invested in heavy industries. The traditional bottom heavy industrial set up was destroyed and instead, Soviet style large industries with thousands of workers at factories and with thousands of peasants in the collective farms producing food for the workforce. This balance could be disturbed with migration and indeed the city life, despite poverty and squalor in them, seemed to hold more promise in terms of food and shelter than what the villages had to give. There was always a danger of farmers marching into the cities and collapsing the food production systems. Hence there was a bar on movement of people, not only from the village to the city but also from one macro region to the other. The restriction on the movement of the people was a way to actually hold people back to fulfil the targets and allocations of planned deployment.

---

[42]Paul Ropp op. cit. 5

The Communist programme is referred to as the Big Push as it was an attempt to plan for the Gross Domestic Product of the country to grow to the levels of the developed world. Mao Zedong, the Chairman of the Communist Party said that he wanted to be able to surpass Great Britain in less than 50 years. The model of economic growth that China pursued during Mao was basically of the style of the Soviet Union to develop heavy industries. The economy was planned at two levels; the prices for inputs were controlled for the large State owned enterprises so that they could procure raw materials at cheaper prices and sell dear once again at controlled output prices. The difference between the revenues and costs were supposed to create surpluses for further investments. This model could have worked very well if there were a slew of downstream industries that could utilize the steel, machinery and chemicals produced out of these factories. Unfortunately too tight a command on the local economy smothered these smaller and indigenous enterprises. The next step was to develop a rural base of industries namely the town and the village enterprises which would help create and circulate wealth locally in smaller regional loops. The two could only meet if the road networks were developed, something which China always had.

The points of difference between Mao and the Nationalist economy lay in the levels of visible parameters of growth rather than in the structure of the economy. While the traditional Chinese economy was "bottom heavy" with numerous producers producing, exchanging, investing and consuming at the household levels, neither Communism nor Nationalism protected this innate structure of Chinese production. Both Nationalism and Communism, in the pursuit of large scale industrialization, heavy industries and development of technology tried to dissolve the bottom heavy structure and instead displaced the households which traditionally functioned as centres of production and instead converted them into suppliers of labour power. This later took a heavy toll on the social fabric of the family and community based Chinese society.

The difference between the Nationalists and the Communists lay in the fact that while the former used foreign capital and especially Japanese capital for developing industries along the Pearl River Delta and the south China Sea coast, the Communists relied on indigenous resources for growing the Chinese economy. Since the local economies could not generate the large quantities of capital, Chinese communists tried to do through labour power what one would have ideally achieved through the use of heavy machinery. Thousands were brought from villages to work in factories, manually lay down roads, damaged by war, and use labour intensive technologies to excavate mineral wealth. In order to feed these thousands, farmers were put into communes, became workers in their own fields and were made to attain unrealistically high targets. Communism concealed a major paradox; namely it gave political power but took away economic power. In many ways the country side became mentally disturbed, community spirit was lost, a mob spirit emerged and production actually fell. Farmers had no incentive to go on producing beyond what the natural farm endowments allowed. Local leaders fudged data, smuggled rations, developed black market and accumulated arms. Governance failed and China immersed into one of the greatest famines human history has ever known in the year 1960. It was clear that the Maoist method of wholly commanding the economy would hardly be of much use[43].

Deng comes in with the failure of the Maoist policies. It was not until the death of Mao that Deng could really emerge from the shadows because Deng's views were at variance to Mao's total command over the economy. There is a broad brush belief that Deng opened China to market economy. This is a simplistic view. There is more to just market in the story of China's growth. It is this story that we will now pursue through the policies of Deng Xiaoping, the Chinese leader in various incumbencies of top positions in the government and the Party between 1978 and 1997[44].

References:

1. Paul.S.Ropp. China In World History.OUP. Oxford. 2011.

---

[43]Frank Dikotter. Mao's Great Famine. Bloomsbury. UK. 2011. Pp 47to 55.
[44]Ezra. F.Vogel. Deng Xiaoping and the Tranformation of China. Harvard University Press. USA. 2011. Pp 217-248.

Chapter Six

What Mao Did Not Do To China

In order to be able to understand the remarkable feat of China
as an economic power, we must start with Mao, one who
is considered to be the very antithesis of economic growth.
Mao's Communism has been translated as one where the
pursuit of equality leaves everyone equally poor in a sharp
contrast to Deng's market economics which allows the free
flow of profits bringing prosperity. Such naïve simplifications
obfuscate the situation in China. China has always been a
world leader in civilization. Just before the Opium Wars
decimated China into a country of rotting millions, China
was the leader of the world in the production of chemicals,
dyes, weaponry, porcelain, utensils, machinery, steel, minerals,
art work, crafts, textiles, wood carvings, printed books,
fruits, vegetables, and processed food stuff like edible oils
and fats. Opium wars defeated and colonized China, cut
across its social relations, disturbed its domestic economy and
impoverished it[45]. It was the mission of both the Nationalists
and the Communists to help restore China to the days of glory.

China has been a tribal country; the essential organization
of the society in China is tribal. This meant that social

---

[45]John Keay, op cit. 6

cooperation has been the key to economic production. The Chinese have also been a materialistic nation where material prosperity has always meant much. The opportunities of the Opium trade created many rich people who drained capital wealth out of the country. It was important for the nationalist movements to divest such exploiters of their power and wealth and instead assume the political control of the state in the hands of the Chinese people. The ruling dynasty, the Qing has been foreigners in the sense that they were Manchurians and the Chinese assigned the reversal of their fates to foreign rule within China. Economic growth was seen to be the key to political sovereignty as much as it was seen as a necessity for overcoming the poverty that most Chinese seem to have fallen into in the aftermath of the control of China by the colonial powers[46].

To understand Mao's programme one must also understand that the decolonization process for China happened through three decades of bitter civil war. The Nationalists fought the Qing, the Communists fought the Nationalists and the numerous revolutionary groups fought one another and the Nationalists and Communists fought the smaller groups to bring them under larger banners. The Communists under Mao wrested powers from the Nationalists driving them into Taiwan while taking control over the mainland. Mao fought the Nationalists from the side of the peasants, driving out the landlord class of Nationalists and capturing the State machinery and the military. Mao's foundation thus was the peasant militarisation. His efforts at

---

[46] Ibid

economic reforms were like raising an army to fight. Despite the constituency of his revolution being the peasant, Mao was initially not enamoured by an agriculture led growth; instead he was keener on the Soviet model of growth that depended upon heavy industries.

Mao started off by emulating the model of development of the Soviet Union with large scale, capital intensive and top heavy industries. China lacked the capital to be able to pay for such an exogenous top down industrialization and hence in a classic textbook manner assuming that labour and capital could continuously substitute each other smoothly Mao substituted labour power for capital investments. Hordes of workers were transported across the country to work on railway lines, roads, bridges, canals, steel mills and other industries. Wages had to be paid and sufficient food had to be produced. The market systems of the Qing age had collapsed on China's closing in and the political economy of autarky, Chinese agriculture huddled together into food self-sufficiency rather than generate marketable surplus. It was a task to extract food for the non-farm people from the farms. The Communist Party with its decentralized and localized cells forced people to work by providing them with targets of production and goading them into community kitchens, hostels and boarding like chattel. In every which way one thinks, such experiments deeply hurt the egos and self-interests of the Chinese people[47].

Mao perhaps never intended his programmes to be as

---

[47]Frank Dikotter, Mao's Great Famine: The History of China's Great Catastrophe, 1958-1962, Bloomsberry, London, 2011.

harsh as they eventually turned out to be; he assumed that the vast mass of the toiling proletariat would have the same level of idealism of equality, participation, economic growth and political sovereignty as he. The spirit of the initial Communism was more of voluntary cooperatives than the forced communes. In the system of the cooperatives, the peasants were required to pool their resources, land, cattle, farming implements, seeds and even money to produce food. But while the system of cooperative farming helped the villages, it did not produce the surplus for the non-food growing population engaged in industry and construction. Surplus had to be forced out of the cooperatives and hence the communes. Under the commune system, land was appropriated by the State, people divided into teams, each required to work according to capacity and receive wages according to needs. The size of families grew due to larger number of children so that "needs" could be inflated and lack of labour excused on account of child rearing. The commune system was not new in China because the Shang and the Qin had it as well and expectedly as in the bygone regimes, the system failed under Mao as well. More the peasants were forced into work, the less the produced plunging China into the Great Famine that ravaged the country between 1958 and 1962, killing nearly 10 million people[48].

Peasants were not inclined to follow the dictates of the Central Command. Besides, farming was a household occupation and not one where peasants were merely converted into workers in lands which they once owned but presently

---

[48]Ibid. pp 230 to 239

has come to be appropriated by the State. The foundation of the Communist regime was land reforms where large private lands were taken away and redistributed among the peasants. The system of forced labour worked well to fatten the pockets of the Party leaders and indeed those close to the Communist Party improved their lot and became quite similar to the very landlords that the Revolution wanted to be displaced. The peasantry was utterly demoralized; they abandoned land and eager to show that they were landless in order to cash on the allowances for the landless and the higher wages in the cities made them migrate to cities as landless labourers that promised a brighter future. Hence redistributed land lapsed back into the hands of the rich who merrily continued to sell grain and food stuff at a premium. Food prices soared, private profits inflated and the State had to raise the price bar higher and higher to induce procurement for the State stocks[49].

The Communist State appropriated land on the one hand and on the other assigned parcels of land to families who worked on it as labour against the payment of wages. Since the communist ethics of paying workers according to needs and not according to productivity did not quite gel with the materialistic and ambitious Chinese, land productivity dropped and food production declined. The State faced a shortage of food for its workers who worked off the land. Migration threatened both urban as well as rural economies where people fled from the village into the cities. Local communist leaders who were in command of community farms known as communes dictated production targets

---

[49]Ibid

and recommended rewards; personal biases, favouritism, corruption in form of illegal sale of grain underlay an economy in which the State could hardly get any surplus from its villages. Hunger stalked China and finally in 1960 the Great Famine peaked and killed nearly 10 million people.

The urgency of China to industrialize emanated from the strains it encountered with the Soviet Union once over Stalin's cold shouldering Mao and then again from Khrushchev's irritation with Mao's attack on Taiwan and fortification along the South China Sea. In a bid to repay the Soviet aid as soon as was possible Mao decided to double, triple and even quadruple China's production in the same way Taiwan had done in order to reduce its dependence upon American aid. The origins of the Famine thus lay also in China's bid to overcome interference of foreign powers in its affairs, "affairs" meaning its attack of Taiwan[50].

Henry Kissinger analyses that China's military aggression is not always provoked by necessities of self-defence. Instead, China operates like its traditional game weiquei, in which the powers are attempted to be held in balance. The ancient Chinese method of soothsaying namely the I Ching is about balancing the evil powers in order to contain and control them. Kissinger notes that unlike in chess, the Chinese do not pursue a total victory. Observed in this way, Chinese aggression may have nothing to do with either its sovereignty or its security but as a means to gain control of powers that surround it[51]. It is important to observe that military might is used liberally in

---

[50]Frank Dikotter, Op cit 47
[51]Henry Kissinger. On China. Penguin. USA. 2001.

China and even in modern times, strategic posturing remains a key to its economic development and economic globalization. China's militarization along the erstwhile Silk Road in a bid to control resources like mineral ore, coal and oil and gas; its military build-up in South America in order to protect its acquisitions in Peru and Brazil vindicates the thesis that for China, military might more than trade facilitation or diplomacy and/or technical partnerships is used to attain economic prosperity.

Just as the peasants rebelled on the ground, similarly, workers in factories also rebelled; in 1956 and 1957, large scale industrial strike dashed Mao's hope of achieving his remarkable targets. Mao also had the dream of China matching up to the Soviet Union; the Chinese hate to be beaten in their own game, socialism in this case and the thought of the Soviet Union comprising of nations, many of who were objects of disdain in China because of their barbarism set Mao into a tizzy of competition. In 1959 when the Soviet Union launched the Sputnik in space, Mao fumed at what he assumed was China's defeat. Almost overnight Mao raised the targets of production, insisted that China should produce at least a quarter of the world's steel which in the late 1950's was 50 million tonnes. Mao designed The Great Leap Forward to attain the unattainable, to overnight convert China into Great Britain and anyone who opposed this programme, albeit on grounds of its practicality was termed as a rightist and persecuted. This led into an inner party dissidence and also was the moment of the birth of a coterie that manifested eventually into the Gang of Four, the core of corruption in

China[52].

Mao's initiated a Cultural Revolution around 1966, raising the slogan of Let Hundred Flowers Bloom. Scholars have read this attempt of Mao to build up a consensus for his programmes by providing space for dissidence. But Mao does not show any kindness towards alternatives to his Great Leap and indeed the secret police, dubbing as rightist anyone who dared to oppose him seems like a paradox to the hundred flower thesis. A possible explanation out of the paradox could be that Mao was once again drawing upon the support of the literary societies and the litterateurs who had once backed up his Party during the war against the Nationalists. More than inviting consensus and appearing to be ideologically accommodating, Mao was actually trying to rebind the spirit of revolution among the literati. The fact Mao never really wanted a consensus and was keen on attaining his targets on the might of the sword was borne by the Red Guards who moved about killing off people, assassinating assumed dissidents especially the students and teachers who seemingly came from "bad social classes", or the upper classes.

The Red Guards were officially called as the People's Liberation Army who took control of the villages and ruled through the barrel of the gun and were particularly effective in the North West provinces. In the city of Shanghai, bands of rebellious youth constituted themselves as Revolutionary Committees and took over civilian authorities. Zhou Enlai was deputed by Mao to negotiate with these Revolutionary Committees; indeed when Zhou Enlai died in 1976, there was

---

[52]Frank Dikotter, Op cit. 47 Pp 8-9 and pg 27.

an enormous gathering at the Tiananmen Square, showing to the world and especially to China that Mao had lost legitimacy to moderates like the dead Zhou. During this phase of his life, Mao found Deng to be the most loyal counter revolutionary leader and brought him to the forefront[53].

Deng's modernization programme was based on the principles expounded by none other than Mao himself. The four pillars were agriculture, industry, science and technology and military.   Agriculture would produce food for the non-producers engaged in industry; science and technology would induce modernism in industry and military might would also draw from the strength of industry and science and technology and would in turn help protect China's influence over economic affairs of the larger civilizational area. China's militarism is not only a matter of self-defence or aggression in order to adopt a certain stance against the hegemony of Soviet Union, USA and Japan but also an active intervention into the economic affairs of countries like Taiwan, Vietnam, and the territory of Hong Kong. Many negotiations regarding investment flows between Hong Kong and Taiwan and mainland China took place over military posturing and sometimes even attacks. Militarism and industrial growth were used by China to free itself of the Soviet domination and the fortification of the South China Sea was clearly linked to the larger issues of trade in minerals and other natural resources. Observed closely Deng's policies are more in continuation with that of Mao's except for a small difference

---

[53]William. A.Joseph. Politics in China - An Introduction. OUP. USA. 2010. Pp 103-129

which lay in agriculture[54].

Mao's economic failure was to assume that people would put collective aims of the revolution ahead of their selfish aims of normal times. His model relied on the assumption that the Communist Party had the full mandate to force people do whatever the Party commanded; Mao assumed that labour could be freely transferred from the village to the city, from farming to construction and from colleges and Universities to factories and administration. People resisted, the infrastructure did not often support such large scale migration and there was simply not enough food in the cities[55]. But this experiment loosened up the Chinese into becoming eager migration and three decades after Mao, it was the free flowing migrant labour that has undoubtedly pulled off the great economic miracle for China.

Mao's unrealistic targets, his attempts to close the gap between Great Britain and China in remarkable short span of time made him forcefully deploy labour into water tight arenas with mindless targets to fulfil. The crash of such a system showed up in China's Great Famine in 1958.

Deng returned land to the household; may be not in terms of titles but at least in terms of allowing families to keep farm surpluses and then use the rest of the produce in a manner they liked. These actually helped families involved in farming increase their production manifold and reinvest the surplus by procuring labour against food wages. While returning land to farming families helped recovers agriculture, the industrial

[54]Ezra F Vogel. Op cit 44, pp 377 to 450.
[55]Frank Dikotter, op cit 43, pp 230 to 241

sector was still very weak. Both Mao and Deng realized the importance of bringing in foreign technology, but unlike Deng, Mao did not open up the economy to trade and foreign joint ventures. Instead, Mao imported foreign technology, primarily from the Soviet Union but for which there was neither the right kind of personnel nor was there the incentive to produce for the global market. Deng opened up the Chinese economy, externally as well as internally so that the foreign investors could invest in economic production and make profits out of the markets.

Factories were of two kinds; the large state owned enterprises and the smaller town and village enterprise. Both suffered enormous losses. With Deng's modernization the loss making State owned enterprises were closed down and trainloads of workers were returned to the villages. It was here that the agrarian surplus helped organize these retrenched workers and make entrepreneurs out of them. Small innovations of electronic torch lights, toys, cheap calculators, and many of such goods were produced en masse across the villages and small towns of China and started to flood markets of the world. Prices were very low because most labour was treated as free; Chinese system of costing is so unlike the Western idea of costs that China can afford to have very different economies whose outward result are the low prices of goods. In this way China produced billions of entrepreneurs all working at frantic paces to assemble television sets, music systems, water purifiers, room heaters, portable dishwashers that swept across the world dislodging local industries and decimating employment. Thousands of small investors went to cities like Shanghai to set up hair cutting saloons, massage parlours, eateries, bakeries and so on. The Chinese entrepreneur wants to make money but also wants the prestige in being in a vocation; in the early days of the Chinese reforms under Deng, it was more to earn the respect as an innovator and an entrepreneur that the millions of self-employed youth sacrificed money profits and made their families to subsidise their experiments by providing for the new entrepreneurs; indeed family support seems to have been the most important social capital that worked[56].

China's economic development did not remain confined to the small and the beautiful but riding the wave upon its millions of entrepreneurs spread into the streets of Singapore, allies of New Delhi and Kolkata, flooded shopping malls in New York and Bonn and inundated the memento shops of almost every tourist destination. The system of the family where peasants grew food to subsidize wages of labour that were often members of the same family and labour subsidized with food, clothing and shelter produced cheap goods and earned cash which was reinvested in further industrialization. Due to the widespread retrenchment of labour by China's State owned enterprises there was a pool of skilled and unemployed but highly employable workers. It is pertinent to note that Deng did not change Mao's priority of putting agriculture first, then heavy industries backed by science and technology and all of this sustained by militarism. What Deng changed in the Maoist approach was to understand a basic

---

[56]Susmita Dasgupta. The TVE Edge. The China Reader. From Mao to the Market. ICFAI. 2001

attribute in the Chinese character; namely the aspiration for material prosperity and family ties[57].

Let us never imagine that the Chinese is an individualistic capitalist; the Chinese is a family person for who the family and the extended kin-group is a source of labour and social capital. The Chinese society expects that surpluses from economic activities should be circulated within the community to procure more labour as direct workers, or as indirect persons carrying goods to cities and across seas. While a rich Chinese is valued for he will have wealth to redistribute, the wealthy Chinese who uses riches only for self-aggrandisement without adequately circulating capital among communities is a paradox in the society. The Qing dynasty, the Silk Road trade, the Opium trade and the colonial trade off cities of Guangdong and Shanghai created a class of selfish merchants who used their newly acquired wealth to purchase goods from outside China, spend money outside the country and thus siphoned off capital from the community. Mao's Communism was a forced return of wealth into the community and attempted to recirculate through the community. In this way, Communism suited China as its civilizational and historical essence.

Deng did not curtail the rich but he tried to lure the wealthy into investing more in businesses that were located in the coastal and southern provinces. These provinces he opened up to the Chinese living in Hong Kong and Taiwan, historically homesick and forever wanting to return to the mainland. Deng used the homesickness of the non-resident Chinese to build up investments in the country. Profits from

---

[57]William A Joseph. Op cit. 53

investments which Taiwan and Hong Kong had accumulated from all over the advanced world were now ready to alight in China to seek its heap and skilled labour. Nearly sixty percent of Chinese exports to the USA actually constituted of Taiwanese and Hong Kongese goods outsourced from China. China's magnificent growth was the absorption of Taiwan's and Hong Kong's prosperity. China's militarism is closely connected to its economic endeavours or joining investment streams of victim countries with that of its own. It attacks islands off the South China Sea; it builds up military bases around Vietnam and Myanmar and threatens them into economic cooperation. Militarism is closely linked to economic exchange; a kind of a forced marriage of the victim's and the victor's economies. This is very different from Japanese aggression which has often been directed at accessing minerals and raw materials from Siberia, Russia, Mongolia, Manchuria and China[58].

Whatever be the mistakes of Mao, his policies did lay a sound industrial base in China. When Mao said that China had to produce as much steel as England did, every householder melted their pots and pans, tore down concrete homes and recovered tor steel to push into rudimentary furnaces to make steel. Most of such steel could not be used because of the appalling quality but nonetheless the people were galvanized into making steel; at least some knowledge and hands on experience was developed which later could be well honed into producing skilled labour. In a bid to industrialize rapidly, the farmers invested whatever they could

---

[58]Martin Jacques. Op cit 17 pp 32-35, 199-201, 357-438.

into building up town and village enterprises, create local infrastructure, network of roads, and transportation so much so that these investments by private peasants constituted nearly 40% of the state investments in public goods and transportations. Mao built up impulses and instincts of the Chinese, rehearsed their responses and reactions to external stimuli; these helped when Deng modernized China.

The Chinese society is based upon strong social networks which grow upon barter exchange of goods and services. Many peasants defied Mao's centralized command economy, smuggled grain out and continued to barter with other kinds of services and goods. Many used surplus grain to send family members out of the village into cities; some helped members to smuggle goods out of villages and sell in cities. Such undercover barter system of exchange steadily built up a demand for industrialized goods and services from the peasants but also created a class of rural elites. This class of rural elites became the nemesis of Mao's centralized command economy and served as the backbone for Deng's reforms.

References:

1. Barry Naughton. The Chinese Economy – Transitions and Growth. MIT. Massachusettes and London. 2006.

2. Frank Dikotter. Mao's Great Famine. Bloomsbury. London. 2010.

Chapter Seven

Principles of Deng's Economic Reforms

The year 1978 has been a watershed year for China; it was the beginning of a new phase of economic reforms in the country. Many scholars are flummoxed at how China could open its economy up to the forces of the market without changing its dictatorial politics. Indeed, when the countries of the erstwhile Soviet Union opened up to neo liberal policies, democracy and demolition of the Communist Party seemed to have preceded such liberalization. In China, it appeared that more the market was liberalized more the Communist Party's hold over the economy was strengthened. The aim of this chapter is to be able to explain this anomaly.

China's modernization under Deng is often known as the "Four Modernizations" because he addressed four segments of the economy, namely agriculture, industry, science and technology and the military. In each of these cases, China has sought the intervention of technology and scientific knowledge, the brilliant enterprises of its people, the social cooperation among its administrative units notwithstanding its wide spread corruption, ad hocism, lack of transparency and tyranny of those in power. Yet, the aim of Deng's modernization does not seem to be the economy; it was more to rein in a political dissent, especially the one as demonstrated at the Tiananmen Square in 1976 at the death of Zhou Enlai. The persistence of rebellion against the Communist Party, the loss of Mao's influence and the ever increasing voices of dissent despite persecution and the PLA conveyed to Deng that in order to keep the authority of the Communist Party over China, one must compromise on economic growth! China's eventual economic growth with Deng's Four Modernizations was initially an attempt at political accommodation of the counter revolutionary groups who opposed Mao, his coterie, his Party, his PLA and his unreasonable demands on the Chinese people[59]. A hundred flowers did bloom with writings, accounts, experiences and art but denouncing Communism and hailing a freer society. Deng's reforms were economic in the shell but political in the kernel.

One never really knows why Deng massacred the protestors at the Tiananmen Square in 1989 because it seems so much like a goal on the same side. It is possible that Deng did not wish to be seen as giving in to the rebels but he revived many of the institutions which were intended at the start of the Communist Revolution. The Party under the leadership of Deng proposed direct election of leaders at the grassroots; villagers were made to read promises and policies. The party abandoned the practice of lifelong incumbency at party posts. The courts and the legal systems were revived;

---

[59]William Joseph. Op cit 53. Pp 103-129

in China, laws are more about upholding mutual agreements and contracts rather than common law or civil law. Funds to the PLA were cut and in many places they were disbanded. Industrialization was decentralized as well, the State Owned Enterprises were scaled down and the Town and Village Industries were attempted to be revived; decentralization was done also to clip the wings of the party bosses who headed the large corporations and power was now devolved lower down to the villages[60].

Traditionally, the Chinese society has been organized in this way since time immemorial and thus Communism in the style that China follows seems to be intrinsic to the society. However, in a bid to develop very quickly and reach Britain's standards in less than a decade, Mao violated a core principle of the Chinese society and which is he imposed the central command instead of having a central road map be coordinated in a series of individual decision making. He forced people to fall in line and thus challenged the very ethos of the Chinese society in which the individual will was coordinated with everyone else's by the central command but not subjugated and surrendered to it. Mao, in a way, treated his people the way the Soviet Union treated it's; for the Soviet Union, the State was a large factory and the people were automatons but for China, the State was a coordinator for the people, each of who was an entrepreneur. Unfortunately for Mao, in his pursuit of farming collectives and production teams and then factory units in all of which peasants and workers were organized in a hierarchy as if in an army, disturbed

---

[60]Ibid

the essentially autonomous people albeit highly aligned to a central authority. Mao's policies of the Great Leap culminated in the greatest famine the modern world has known so far. Deng initiated reforms in which the individuals were allowed to become entrepreneurs again. This is how he organized his reforms.

On the agrarian front, Deng reverted back to the household responsibility system for farmers. Mao had appropriated all farming lands into State ownership and peasants were made to work as labourers against payment of wages and not being allowed to retain surpluses. This reduced incentives to work hard and soon people were looking to move away from fields into cities where workers often got assured access to housing and food. Mao's reforms were not merely imposed from above but an outcome of a popular mandate which was at the base of Communism. In order to check social inequality, which creates social conflict, an anathema to the Chinese society that extols cooperation, Mao initiated land reforms. Land was taken from the rich landlords, most of who had made money out of the Opium Trade and redistributed to the poor. But the situation was such that while the poor could cultivate on land they found that the surplus generated from it did not enable them to do anything else to get a good life, namely health, education and housing. Peasants resold land to those from whom land had been taken away and migrated into cities to work in factories. The cities, in order to attract workers offered several incentives like subsidized food, health and housing. But such mass migration and land alienation would have deepened the very social inequality which Mao and his

Communism wanted to fight. Thus was passed the rule that no peasant could leave land and enter the cities. One needed to have permits to live in the city and back home; all farmers were to receive wages for their labour on farm. In this way, social inequality was to be contained and food production to be increased.

The above plan failed. Unlike in the Soviet Union, where there was a history of feudalism and statist determinism, China was more tribal and hence egalitarian in organization. Though the Western historians often comment on China's lack of democracy, it is far from true that Communism is as totalitarian in China as it is often believed to be. In fact, in China, Communism is a means of ensuring social equality and a way of reinvesting surpluses in gathering labour power for various investments in community goods. Social capital rather than physical capital is China's path of accumulation and Communism helps ensure the accumulation of social capital. But in Mao's model, also inspired much by Stalinism, the fiercely independent and entrepreneurial Chinese was made to work as a mere cog in a large assembly line of production. This is where Mao failed and with a drop in food production across the country, China drowned in the severest famine that the modern world has ever witnessed.

Deng did not return land to peasants but allowed them to retain occupation and the right of cultivation. The peasants rather than the communes would now pay taxes to the State and then be allowed to retain whatever he would produce. This came to be known as the Household Responsibility System. This helped barter among the peasants who then used surplus food to procure labour power and to invest in small businesses in cities, especially Shanghai. In fact, the surplus food that the peasants produced, now with the incentives of being allowed to retain surpluses helped the village communes to redeploy the workers retrenched from the State Owned enterprises in cities into the various town and village enterprises those were lying closed and inoperative for quite a while. The first flush of industrialization and rapid economic growth came, not from the investments in outsourced businesses of the Pearl River Delta but from these small but numerous town and village enterprises spread across the interiors of China. It was this stratum of decentralized decision makers who eventually became the strongest voice to demand democracy[61].

China under Mao followed some textbook formulae for bringing about economic growth and one such manifestation was to transfer labour from agriculture to industry in order to increase productivity in both. This resulted in a mass scale forced transfer of labour from villages into cities and later erecting many barriers for subsequent migration into the cities. It was as if, China wanted to maintain optimum labour supply in agriculture, industry and the services. It was imagined that the only way in which labour productivity could rise in land was to ease land of overcrowding with disguised unemployment. Huge State Owned Enterprises of heavy industry were created in order to absorb the surplus labour. Unfortunately the scheme failed. The migration of labour from

---

[61] Barry Naughton. The Chinese Economy - Transitions and Growth. MIT. USA. 2007 pp 88-95.

agriculture to industry is an outcome of development and not an engine of the same; development happens with surplus in farms which are then invested into industry by creating a food pool to feed workers who need not produce food and can focus on industry instead. Mao tried to move labour before a surplus was produced in land. He tried to create a ready to occupy industrial structure which did not necessarily emanate out of surpluses accumulated out of farmlands. Mao lost the key of improving agrarian productivity.

On the other hand, Deng returned to the peasant household, allowed them to retain surpluses from their own production and use the surplus in a manner in which they desired, albeit after paying up the usual taxes. Instead of appropriating surpluses and then redistributing the same to allocate labour force variously in industry and agriculture, the way Mao's Communism worked, Deng actually let the people redistribute the surpluses in a similar manner in order to allocate the labour power of the members of their families and communities into farms, or industries or even in restaurants, curio shops or saloons in the cities. Deng calls this principle as market mechanism with socialism; market because the individual agents take the decisions and socialism because surpluses are used to engage more labour from within the community on the principle of barter and exchange. This model of exchanging food and labour power is intrinsic to the Chinese society as well as a basic principle of socialism because this model focusses the engine of growth on social capital rather than physical or financial capital. Hence, Deng's thesis of market socialism is a return to the basic nature of the

Chinese people and society[62].

While Deng launched his economic reforms from the principles of market socialism rooted fundamentally on agriculture yet not all his reforms were socialistic in nature. He encouraged business outsourcing, invited high technology capital growth and built up his model of Pearl River Delta where foreign companies could use the cheap Chinese labour and heavily subsidised infrastructure to produce goods to dominate global markets. These reforms that encouraged high tech industries with very high quality products suddenly seemed to oppose the growth story of China through the several town and village enterprises, counterfeit brands, cheap electronic products and various levels of innovations in toys, games, and household items. The global capital and the local capital, both freed now were at loggerheads.

The possible reasons for the conflict could have been in the competitive nature of the Chinese people and the use of culture and ideology as a mode of social domination. Those in villages and provinces located in the mainland now could see people in the Pearl River Delta region flourishing thanks to the investments flowing in from Taiwan and Hong Kong. The people from the interior, who were hitherto the higher echelons of the society and looked down upon the coastal people as not being Chinese saw the latter rise in economic prosperity. Pressures built up in Deng to equalize the situation, which Deng did to an extent when he favoured Shanghai over the Delta, but as for taking this high technology growth inwards, Deng did not care much. Thus

_____
[62]Ibid 231

while village based market socialism may have been Deng's foundation for reforms, it appeared that he had another copybook neoliberal model for Shanghai and the Pearl River Delta. After 1989, Deng started pursuing a clearer policy of neoliberalism. In order to pursue neoliberalism in its purer form, Deng embarked upon authoritarianism, something he needed in order to be able to channelize bank credit and other financial incentives to the high tech large units. The centralized command over the economy was maintained just in order to favour the bigger players. Corruption erupted over favouritism and discretion that central command brought with it and one could sense many frauds where companies sank funds or fled the scene aided by government favours. The continued government controls for the State owned sector led to dual pricing, inflation, black market and rampant corruption. China started executing corrupt officials without restraint and mobile execution vans plied the streets of cities; but such executions became means of personal vendetta rather than social justice and hence served no purpose. But despite its pitfalls, China grew and grew boundlessly and limitlessly and true to its long held dream today China commands half of all the world's resources and controls the same amount of global markets[63].

Much has been written about the dual track and the dual pricing system of China. Scholars often look upon this as a way in which the semblance of socialism was maintained while promoting the market forces. This is not quite the case.

---

[63]Dambisa Moyo, Winner Take All - China's Race For Resources and What It Means For Us. Penguin. Great Britain. 2007.

The dual pricing was a system where the SOEs had to sell a certain quantity of their produce at controlled prices and could sell the rest at market prices. The aim of the dual pricing was to ensure cheap and subsidized inputs for other SOEs and then to increase productive capacities for the markets, especially the export market. In a later chapter, it has been discussed how China actively promoted areas around the coast for purposes of export oriented units. With the dual pricing system, Deng was not exactly in a mood to keep up the stance of socialism; instead it was a way to further strengthen the SOEs vis-à-vis the TVEs[64].

When Deng said market socialism, he actually meant two very different things. For the peasants and the entrepreneurs of the interior mainland, it meant that individuals took the decisions of what to produce and whom to produce and to procure the inputs for production from within the society by developing social networks, barter and mutual exchange. For the larger State owned units, market meant the freedom to hire and fire and to set prices while socialism meant the retaining the state control over these units. In other words, for the town and village enterprises there was no ownership control but they operated within the domestic market. For the larger units, they could change prices but neither ownership nor production decisions though the government gave substantial autonomy to the managers of these units. They could hire and fire and thus do away with the security of employment that the Chinese workers were so used to.

The sense of insecurity rose in China and people rushed

---

[64]Barry Naughton op cit. 61

to save more and more of their earnings, or invest into real estate which they could dissolve in times of crisis. The real estate boom in China and wherefrom it spread to the rest of the world has sustained much of China's money circulation. But the Keynesian paradox of savings goaded China and its consumption suffered at the hands of reckless savings. Foreign trade came to the rescue. But the pursuit of foreign trade had its own problems. Since over 50% of the production of the basic industrial raw materials was supplied through the SOEs and an equal amount of infrastructure and basic utilities controlled by them, the rest of the economy consisting of smaller producers and local level town and village enterprises suffered when they wanted to export their goods. Also, Deng's favouritism towards the coastal areas made the people from the interior upset because they had to encounter various tolls and port fees, enhanced in rates.

The officers of the SOEs and other government agencies embarked on lucrative trade on the side by smuggling and selling raw materials to the ever ready market of decentralized industrial units. This led to corruption on the one hand but incurred losses for the SOEs. Deng decided to decentralize the units. The roots of decentralization were the losses of the SOEs and this eventually adversely impacted the public expenditure on health and education. Consequently these suffered. As householders had to pay more and more for health and education they started spending less and less and saving more and more bringing upon China repeatedly the paradox of savings a la Keynes. The raise in public expenditure became crucial. China compensated for a drop in state revenues by further opening up to FDIs and foreign trade.

Foreign trade in China is not the same as international trade elsewhere in the world. In China, trade is controlled by large State owned trading corporations who buy at global prices and then sell at exorbitant prices in the domestic market and thus makes neat margins. Often Chinese domestic goods are procured at miserably poor rates but sold elsewhere at higher prices again bringing in profits for the trading companies. For some time foreign trade only fattened the pockets of the trading companies and created personal wealth for those in charge of these companies. While before the 1980's these revenues were sources of funds for the Communist Party, after Deng's liberalization by which SOEs obtained managerial freedom, the Party has less control of profits. The ancient motif of merchant versus the Emperor seemed to return and Deng was, as expected not too happy with the activities of the Foreign Trade Companies. The only way out for Deng to discipline the profiteering of these companies was to have China enter the WTO.

In 1996-97, China prepared itself to enter into the WTO. A nation known for undercutting exports to gain market shares especially in the developed world perhaps surprised many of us with its commitments to remove subsidies and other protectionist measures. Also, China's system of accounting has been unique because not all kinds of costs are reflected in manufacturing because of the barter system that still dominates so much of China's economy. As a step to bring China into the fold of a western system of accounting, Deng introduced the Value added tax and the service tax. This was yet another move to promote the foreign owned firms and the State owned enterprises in the country over the town and village enterprises. Deng wanted China to emerge at par with the West and had little need for its indigenous industry; the interior could produce food and supply labour while the coast and Shanghai could have its industries, modern, global and multinational.

In yet a series of reforms for the WTO, China had to also set up many financial institutions and do away with import tariffs. There was a substantial reduction of tariffs on imported inputs but the banks, though expanded in the scope of operations in terms of segments they could lend to, but as long as the banks controlled the lending according to a single central plan, many products of import substitution were promoted. However with a remarkable decrease in tariff rates and a virtual elimination of quantitative restrictions, the Chinese government also abolished the dual pricing system. All commodities were brought into the same market while China also followed the current account currency convertibility. These reforms were completed by 1997 and the Chinese economy became aligned to the requirements of the WTO.

Deng wanted China to earn foreign exchange through exports; he followed a policy of protecting the domestic industry from imports and to promote exports as well. Exports earned revenues but also required raw materials something which the State owned enterprises either supplied at very high prices or not at all except in the black market. Deng was forced also to open up imports. This was yet another impulse towards further liberalization. The challenge was now not so much of how to maintain the control of the State over its enterprises but how to enable and empower these units to be market friendly and delivery oriented. But the market could not be allowed to dominate alone because most of the State owned industries where foreign investments were to be received were steeped in losses. These losses were sought to be made up by "planned economy". Hence we have full State control over bank credit and the continuation of dual pricing so that the State owned enterprises could get an unfair advantage. In the extension of state control in the name of planning, the government tried to eliminate the smaller players, mainly in the form of town and village enterprises. No wonder then the movement for democracy was also a shadow battle between the small and the large enterprises, the local and the provincial and the State sector for the control of the economy.

In order to encourage the State owned enterprises, Deng invited foreign capital. Foreign capital took advantage of the Chinese labour markets. China has a large population who are ever ready to migrate from the village to the city, fond of city life and urban culture and willing to work for wages even while they were lower than anywhere else in the world. China despite being a communist country had really reduced labour rights; and if the enterprise was foreign owned then it need not adhere to any laws on employment and wages whatsoever. In fact, a huge lay off of labour force from the State owned enterprises when the latter was being restructured supplied the large skilled manpower for the interior zones of the town and village enterprises. Barry Naughton reports that between

1993 and 2004 almost 50 million people lost their jobs in China and as jobs in the formal economy were declining too, one assumes that most workers were reemployed in the informal sector[65]. The urban informal sector grew in China on the might of supply of labour force in the form of retrenched workers but at the same time, there is a social divide among the migrants and the entrenched, the latter of who are usually employed in the formal sector. The urban formal workers have higher incomes while the migrants in the informal sector have lower incomes often supported by farm incomes back home. These migrants into the city often build a bridge between the rural China and urban China carrying the benefits of urbanization back into the rural areas and creating vents for farm surpluses in urban informal trades.

China has been remarkable for the growth of savings which has legendarily sponsored its economic expansion programme. While the common opinion lauded the rise in the Chinese rates of savings, what one missed was the source of such savings. The household was the prime mover of savings; uncertain employment, near total absence of social security, high dependence on family funds and the state of underdevelopment of investment avenues as in the stock markets, raised levels of savings[66]. The subsequent liberalization of banking and finance was to extend debt instruments into the household sector to capture its savings for the large scale enterprises under State ownership. The

---

[65]Ibid, pp 185-187
[66]Pranab Bardhan. Awakening Giants Feet of Clay - Assessing the Economic Rise of China and India. OUP. Delhi. 2012. Pg 67

impulse towards the market came from two sources; one was the attempt of banks to include the household savings, which also meant that the smaller and independent entrepreneurs obtained more loans for businesses[67]. Secondly, the larger State owned enterprises needed end users which again were the town and village enterprises which Deng wanted to suppress. Loans were now extended to such processing and downstream industries that consumed the products of the larger state owned units. Thus, the savings from the interior, yellow zone and the end use and downstream industries also of this region was the main impulse of the Chinese expansionary economic policies.

For minds used to the Western idea of banking, the nature of the Chinese banking system might be difficult to grasp. Banking is an ancient Chinese institution and has its origins right back in Buddhism. Banks helped merchants to transport goods from one place to another without having to carry cash or coins. Fear of dacoits lurked everywhere and loot and theft were common place. Banks thus were custodians of money and issued certificates. Since trade was proliferative in China since ancient times, banks too existed. In fact, China is the originator of paper money. The banks would charge the customers for safe keeping of its money. The idea of bank lending in order to promote investments is alien to the Chinese civilization and indeed to almost the whole of the Oriental civilization. Liberalization of banks did not perform the role that Deng expected them to do precisely because culturally

---

[67]Ted C.Fishman. China Inc - The Relentless Rise of the Next Great Superpower. Simon and Schuster. London 2005. Pp 59-61.

they were not oriented to building projects. Banks did exactly what they were supposed to do in China; be the custodian of money. This strange behaviour of the banking system has created interesting possibilities for extending economic activities. Chinese firms do not take away the proceeds from exports to a country and instead use the money to procure goods for import into their country. This is exactly how China started its trade with India since 2003. Chinese traders exported large quantities of various kinds of goods and used the proceeds to buy up iron ore which China demanded in large quantities in order to expand steel production. The frantic buying of minerals from across the world by Chinese traders took place because they did not repatriate revenues back into China and instead used it to source goods from purchasing countries.

Three kinds of banks were set up in China in order to match up with financial liberalization; the export import bank, industrial development bank and agricultural and financing bank. These steps were supposed to ensure the development of a competitive money and capital market in China. With the establishment of such banks, the earlier policies of selective credit were discontinued and banks now had the autonomy of financing businesses. These developments took a while to fructify and by the year 2002-03, there developed in China a mammoth scale of speculative foreign trade in commodities. Chinese importers purchased half of the world's minerals, gobbled up steel and metals and created a pool of people with Chinese currencies who then bought Chinese goods. For countries in North America and Western Europe which did not have minerals and metals to export to China and only imported goods from China, the latter bought bonds and securities in these countries. Much of the present crisis in the Eurozone is also due to China not reinvesting securities back into these economies. Such imbalances that China creates in the world by attempting to control the whole of its economy will put a question mark on whether its growth will be sustainable[68].

It is possible to draw a timeline for the path of economic reforms in China.

1. 1976, defeat of the Gang of Four and the rise of Deng Xiaoping as the Chinese premier. Deng revives the Chinese dream of modernization and world domination. He realizes that the market and not Maoism can help China rise to heights.

2. Deng plays on the Chinese aspirations to be entrepreneurs. Returns land to peasant families through the Household Responsibility System. This helps peasants to keep most of their surplus with them and invest the same in a manner they like. In the first instance farmers used surplus to procure labour and reinvigorate the TVEs or to set up small shops in the cities.

3. Deng intensified marketization a bit more in order to lure farmers to sell more and more food into the

---

[68]Dambisa Moyo. Winner Take All - China's Race For Resources and What It Means For Us. Penguin. Great Britain.2012.

market. As a corollary of this step, Deng put the TVEs into a relative disadvantage by actively promoting and favouring the State Owned Enterprises. Farmers would sell food in the market if profits from reinvesting the surplus would yield lower profits.

4. Deng wanted more food in the market precisely because he wished to raise wages. Deng was looking for workers while the Chinese aspired to be entrepreneurs. This was actually the model of Maoist development but Deng used the basic instincts of the Chinese to invest surpluses out of farming to procure similar effects of industrial development.

5. Deng develops the Pearl River Delta region in order to integrate China into the globalized economies of Taiwan and Hong Kong. Cheaper wages in the mainland was intended to pull in outsourced industries into China.

6. The policy of developing the Pearl River Delta created resentments within the Party and soon Deng was forced to show discriminatory favours towards Shanghai over the Pearl River Delta regions.

7. However, Deng's policy of favouring the large industry over the smaller home grown ones provoked a new politics for democracy. Through the demand for democracy, the local and provincial governments wanted more powers to be able to control production, movement of goods and people. Deng's policies brought about the lure of the city and migration of the Chinese away from

the village to the city emptied villages of young persons and enterprises collapsed. Democracy ensured local powers.

8. Deng's insistence on Communism paradoxically promoted the cause of the market driven neoliberalism.

9. All through the 1980's and much of the 1990's, China's economy grew out of the skills of the local entrepreneurs. As long as they concentrated on enterprises such as small manufactures such as umbrellas, zippers, toys, bags, assembled electronic items there was no problem. But once these enterprises tried to move up as in tool production and more sophistication and required raw materials, bank finance and wider marketing networks, they encountered many difficulties.

10. Chinese products were cheap because the food for workers was subsidized in the sense that it was home grown and non-traded. China conquered the world on the basis of such cheap goods. But China decided that it would enter into the WTO in the early 1990's. This would require China to adopt a whole new process of accounting. Interestingly, this would also mean a new way of operating. China used a lot of social capital in setting up businesses. Local "arrangers" would locate raw materials, link up markets, place orders and then procure the output. These "arrangers" had little sense of accounting. But China's entry into the WTO would change these and especially the power of the arrangers.

11. China's entry into the WTO was necessary because Deng insisted on inviting outsourced foreign firms instead of promoting the local Chinese business. Also, for China to grow one needed a steady flow of raw materials. Despite many kinds of administrative reforms and financial restructuring of the State Owned Enterprises, a steady supply of raw materials and inputs could not be ensured except through imports.

12. Entry into the WTO meant that the import tariffs would be lowered and this would promise a wider variety of inputs especially for the local industries. A larger access to inputs also dictated Chinese change in economic policy from an import substitution industrial policy towards an export led growth.

13. In the 1980's, some kind of a credit union had developed in the rural areas. These unions helped enterprises grow at an enormous pace. These unions mushroomed and covered almost the whole of interior China. Initially they transacted business among themselves and extended credit to one another albeit within a limited area. Later they expanded and many became cooperative banks and even stockholding companies.

14. These unions played very important role in developing industry and in some cases urbanizing villages by investing in infrastructure. Since poor infrastructure in cities was becoming a hindrance to China's continued growth and much of development in China relied upon

social capital where residents themselves developed local infrastructure, these credit unions became very important in China.

15. Banking reforms were attempts at reigning in such rooted growth in China, something that gave importance to the individuals and local cadres and leaders and threatened the monopoly of the Party and its leaders.

From the above path of reform, it is clear that China's reforms were targeted not at economic sectors but at political constituencies. Deng freed the farmer first, from where possibilities of rebellion have always come first and from where during the 1970's rebellion against the Communist Party was imminent. Mao's policies had reduced the proud peasant to a mere automaton, a beggar, a vagabond living under the charity of the State. But Deng restored the peasant to his pride. The empowered peasant now absorbed much of the retrenched workers from the failing SOEs (state owned enterprises) in the revived TVEs (town and village enterprises) and helped reign in some discontent. As the TVEs grew in power and placed China in the global map of cheap electronic products, imitation consumer brands of the West and even in tools and machine parts, the captains of the SOEs got envious and fearful that investments might flow into these villages away from their units. A slew of policies later developed which actually put the interior down in order to promote the SOEs.

References:

1. Barry Naughton. The Chinese Economy – Transitions and Growth. MIT Press. Massachusettes and London. 2006.

2. Ted. C.Fishman. China. Inc – The Relentless Rise of the Great Superpower. Simon and Schuster. UK. 2005.

3. Ch. Rajeswar (ed). The Chinese Odyssey. Institute of Chartered Financial Analyst. Hyderabad. 2001.

4. Ezra.F. Vogel. Deng Xiaoping and the Transformation of China. Harvard University Press. USA. 2011.

5. Richard Bernstein and Ross H Munro. The Coming Conflict With China. Vintage Books. New York. 1998.

6. Willem Van Kemenade. China, Hong Kong and Taiwan Inc – The Dynamics of a New Empire. Vintage Books. New York. 1998.

Chapter Eight

Deng and Democracy

After the wave of reforms swept through the mainland China in the 1990's, the good and the bad effects of Deng's reforms started surfacing one after another. A first there was the dichotomy between the "bureaucratic and xenophobic" North and "cosmopolitan and commercial south". The resistance of Guangdong in the South to Beijing's centralism in the North became more pronounced. Emboldened by a Southern coalition between Guangdong and Hong Kong and with Hainan Fijian and far more populous but poor interior provinces, policy makers and people preferred to veer towards the south where scope was created not only by investors but also by migrant labour. The south eastern zone became a haven of hope for unemployed workers, displaced peasants, and aspiring youth and emerged in the popular psyche as succour. Such developments created conditions for the rise of democratic forces. Deng paradoxically opposed this.

It is not that Deng did not make any efforts at democratization. He did start the system of elections at the grassroots which decided on local representatives but did not allow a say in national affairs. Deng was anxious that were democracy to be allowed across China, provinces like Tibet and Xinjiang might claim Independence. China did not allow free movement of persons from one location to another; the Mao regime did not allow peasants to come away from land and there were restrictions on urban living. Such restrictions on the movement of labour were needed to control the flow of labour into productive activities; clearly democracy would have been detrimental to such restrictions.

It appears that the workers, peasants, retired persons, housewives, students and other commoners were eager for democracy under Deng just as they had once been eager for communism under Mao. But the ruling elites, investors, managers of large enterprises and party workers did not want democracy. The Chinese society was class divided; the upper class who wanted to continue with the authoritarian structures and the lower classes who wished to bring in democracy. Intellectuals who attempted to raise the bogey of democracy threatened to step into the shoes of the Communist Party and threaten its position. The intellectuals therefore were looked upon as the ones who wished to usurp power from the Communist Party. Being educated abroad, intellectuals for democracy posed a threat to the ruling gentry by raising people's voices and taking their sides and demanding power to rule. The Tiananmen Tragedy took place as a result of a brutal crushing of the pro-democracy forces in China in 1989. By 1989, China's one child policy had taken shape and most families had only single children. Families spent enormously on children's education and hence expected a lot from the future. Several relatives could often pool in money to educate a single ward to see her through to medical college or an engineering course. Educated children were looked upon as ones who could enter the elite society and improve the lot of the entire family. Students' protests were thus taken very seriously in China and students obtained immediate public sympathy and support. Hunger strikes by children made the society grow very concerned. The society and the Party were headed for direct collision.

The Tiananmen Tragedy of 1989 was a brutal repression by the Chinese State of a peaceful protest by students, white collared employees and workers in the Tiananmen Square in Beijing. A movement mainly led by students demanded a multi-party rule to replace the dictatorship of a single party, to develop institutions of the state to overreach the will of the Party and to have less bureaucratic control over the market. One wonders whether Deng was also not part of the Maoist thinking that suspected the power of the well to do people in the affairs of China? Did he also fear the power of the intelligentsia as a class whose interests the pro-democracy movement projected? Did Deng feel that while China needed democracy if only to soften the force of anti-Mao rebellions, he could not allow the Communist Party and the State to wholly lose control over the economy and hence the society?

The hunger strike manifesto read, "We are on hunger strike!! We protest! We appeal! We repent! Death is not what we seek; we are searching for true life." Chinese intellectuals must dispose of their old age disease, passed down over centuries, of being spineless, of merely speaking, not acting. By means of action, we protest against military control, by means of action, we call for birth of a new political culture and by means of action, we express our repentance for wrongs that we have been doing of our own age old weaknesses. The Chinese nation has fallen behind, for this each one of bears his share of responsibility." In another wall poster the students appealed to all Chinese from those in the government down to every ordinary citizen, to give up the old political culture and begin a new one. The movement for democracy got an unprecedented support from all quarters; subscriptions, food, drinks, rain gear, paper, medicines poured in. As the number of protestors increased by the day, professionals like doctors, bankers, lawyers, teachers, nurses, housewives, pensioners all joined in. The gatherings at Tiananmen swelled to a million. It was this million that tanks and guns of the Chinese Army crushed. The movement was quelled.

It is possible that the nothing in concrete terms was gained from the movement; but it instilled a sense of confidence, interdependence, and civility among the Chinese people. Oliver Schell and David Shambaugh write in their book, The China Reader[69] that the movement changed the socio-psychological attributes of the Chinese, from an uncritical acceptance of the Party authoritarianism to discourses against Communism and then into a political consciousness that revolted against corruption, authoritarianism, ad hoc ism and tyranny. Just around this time, there were a lot of discussions especially in the US about the growing violation of human rights in China. Fang Lizhi, a Chinese intellectual was invited on behalf of all the Chinese intellectuals to the US, which angered Deng and created angst among the Party against

[69]China Reader, op cit 56, pg 194

students and the intellectuals.

The event that triggered the Tiananmen uproar was probably the death of Hu Yabong, a leader who was relatively the most popular leader of the Communist Party. Hu Yabong, a leader of the Cultural Revolution and then a Deng loyalist had often been purged and recalled and the purged again both by Mao and Deng for his penchant for over enthusiasm and personalization of programmes. On Hu Yabong's death, his fans wrote on his grave stone, "the one who should be living is dead while those who live on should have been dead." Needless to say the last referred to Deng. Hu Yabong's appeal to the students was that he was one who openly mentioned that he had no attachment towards China's archaic culture and history. Hu's mourning procession took a political character and Deng's position appeared to be genuinely threatened. Deng decided to wait for the burial and the mourning period to be over and then start his military offensive against his own people.

Around the time of the revolt in the Tiananmen Square in 1989 there were two important visitations in China. One was of George Bush the senior from the US who commented on the violations of human rights in China while the other was from Gorbachev, the Soviet Premier. The Soviet Union Premier was visiting China after years of cold relations. Deng was eager to show off to Gorbachev, the victory of Communism; a movement for democracy was detrimental to this image, while the brutality in crushing popular forces by a Communist government was even worse. In the mass movement against inflation in 1986, Hu had tackled the protests with such a humane face and in the spirit of cooperation that when in 1989, after Hu was no more, Deng crushed the movement fiercely, sentiments against the latter surged. Deng and Li Peng were in favour of harsh repression while the recently deposed Premier Zhao Ziyang supported the rebels. The Tiananmen movement served as a platform for party leaders to fight their personal and ideological battles over. The repression had to be lethal because it was, for Deng, a shadow fight for power within the party, something which he was in no mood to lose to the liberals.

Interestingly, during the Communist Revolution the society was divided vertically between the Nationalists and the Communists. But the democratic revolution seemed to have divided the society laterally; the winners of liberalization supported authoritarianism while the losers supported democracy. Also, the Chinese ruling elite, especially Deng did not believe that the masses could actually pull off the economic liberalization programme and hence too much power in their hands could pathetically jeopardize the case for the economic expansionism in the country. Interestingly, China's industrial base has been founded upon its billions of entrepreneurs and yet its politics does not believe in incorporating the will of the people. Hence, despite China's modernization in industry and science and technology, modernization of media and social mores, its polity remains tied to the ancient ideas of Mandate of Heaven without helping the people to develop as citizens of a Republic.

When one looks at the four Asian tigers, namely Singapore, Hong Kong, Taiwan and South Korea, one observes that these countries have also transformed into democracies under the influence of the US interventions; China has resisted democracy precisely because it sees in this effort attempts at Western powers to spread its influence. After the experience of the Opium War where Western powers decimated the great civilization of China and rendered it into an opium addicted poor country, the Chinese were wary of western influences especially ones like democracy which would have changed the Chinese character from passivity and docility and subservient to central authority into one like the individualistic European or American. China does not believe in giving voice to the people; workers are not given their rights, consumer rights are not recognized either and in an overall manner China has the world's worst human rights records.

While China does not allow democracy, the civil society appears to have gained some space. Deng insisted that the Chinese system of moving by consensus does not allow for multi-party system and contested views. But economic growth also brings about political pluralism and the rise of civil society in China answered this need of pluralism. The civil society, especially Green Peace campaigned against the Three Gorges Dam and other such developmental programmes which only helped private capital but were ecologically damaging. The Chinese government did not like these developments. The civil society also gained space in the Chinese nationals directly claiming compensation from the Japanese government for the germ attacks by Japan on China during the WWII[70]. Many civil society groups complained

---

[70]China Daily reports in http://english.people.com.cn/200507/20/
eng20050720_197262.html#. In August, 2002 the Tokyo District Court
dismissed claims for compensation from 180 Chinese victims and relatives of
deceased victims of the germ warfare carried out by the infamous Unit 731 of
the Japanese army, based near Harbin, capital of north eastern Heilongjiang
Province.
The Chinese claimants demanded US$84,000 each and an apology from the
Japanese Government.
The court acknowledged, for the first time, that the Japanese army waged
germ warfare in China during and before World War II.
At that time, the district court rejected the lawsuit, saying "no international
law that enables individuals to sue for war damages had been established at
the time or has been now."
The court used post-war treaties as an excuse for not paying compensation to
the victims of the Imperial Japanese army's reprehensible treatment of the
Chinese.
No international laws exempt Japan from its war responsibilities.
Unit 731 perpetrated the most shocking, heinous, cruel crime the civilized
world has ever known - it used human beings for vivisection to develop
biological weapons.
Both chemical and biological warfare were banned by the Geneva Convention
of 1925. Totally disregarding international laws and human morality, Unit
731 released fleas infected with bubonic plague and food dosed with cholera
bacteria in Zhejiangand Hunan provinces between 1940 and 1942, killing at
least 10,000 people.
Recently a few former members of Unit 731, regardless of pressure from the
Japanese Government, resolutely stood up to bear witness to the truth for
posterity.
The volume of testimony on the activities of Japan's germ warfare in China
has failed to touch the stone heart of Japan. Japan has cited over the years the
1972 China-Japan joint communique to clear its conscience over responsibility
for the fate of Chinese nationals.
The Chinese Government declared it would give up its war reparations from
Japan in 1972 when China and Japan forged diplomatic relations.
The Japanese revisionists take the clause in the joint communique as
justification to offload their country's war obligations, including paying
reparations to individual victims.
From 1937 through to 1945, Japan's aggression cost 11 million Chinese lives
and caused China a loss of US$300 billion US$120 billion from the government
and US$180 billion from individuals.
When the Chinese Government waived its claims for compensation from
Japan in 1972, individuals were not included. The document does not deprive
victimized individuals and their relatives of the right to request an apology

of the Japanese apathy and demanded compensation aggressively. Such groups helped people to raise their levels of civic consciousness and infuse a sense of individual agency.

With the growth of the civil society there was a religious revival as well. Many Churches were opening across China and with many Taoist and Buddhist following suit and the Chinese government attacked these perhaps drawing upon the memory of the Taiping Rebellion and the White Lotus movements. The Taiping Rebellion was a massive uprising mainly by peasants across China who drew upon Christian morals and was inspired by Protestantism. The White Lotus movement was before the Taiping Rebellion and was instrumental in upsetting imperial dynasties in China before the Qing, the last empire before the Nationalist and Communist uprising. These historical memories made the Chinese government very anxious to nip such movements in the bud.

However, as mentioned earlier, in Deng's time, the process of democratization had already begun at the village level by replacing appointed or nominated with elected

---

and compensation from Japan.

Most of the treaties drawn up after 1945 make a clear division between governmental and individual claims for war reparations. It is common practice that the individuals' right to claim war compensation is not covered by their government's right.

Chinese leaders have made this clear on various occasions. According to China's Constitution, the government cannot represent Chinese nationals to waive claims for war compensation until the National People's Congress approves such a move, which it has never done.

When Chinese nationals request war reparations from the Japanese Government, they ask for justice.

History is a heavy page Japan will not be able to turn over if the country refuses to face it squarely.

representations. The directly elected village councils could now elect the representatives of Municipal People's Congress, which again elects the representatives of the Provincial People's Congress. The National Council members were elected by the members of the Provincial People's Congress. In this way the 1 million villages in China experienced some kind of elections though not a multiparty system. However the Chinese villages do not follow any standard procedures for conducting elections. Methods of election vary from province to province. However, maintaining the culture of consensus the incumbent council resigns en masse if new candidates appear for more than a fifth of the positions in the council. A possible reason for opposing democracy in China by the Communist party could be that democracy rests upon individualism and it was feared that collective decisions might be taken through numbers in a rights based individualism of democracy rather than the consensus upon which the Chinese society is based.

Also a compelling reason why Deng opposed democracy was rampant corruption. Family clans, mafia, obscure religious sects and much kind of bands of men and women operated to sabotage government programmes in the country side. Also the "peasant phobia" loomed large across the countryside where it was possible for peasant rebellions to have erupted at any point of time. China has known violent peasant uprisings which have often dislodged empires and changed fortunes of the imperial incumbents. Deng worked out of this historical memory and feared that should the peasants be given more powers through democracy, the central rule of the Communist Party would be jeopardized. Besides, the urbanites were not eager to open Chinese villages and peasants to political decentralization because the economies of the metropolitan centres like in Guangdong, Shanghai and other regions of the Pearl River Delta producing high value and high technology goods were in direct conflict with the town and village enterprises that produced low value and low technology goods. It was here that Deng feared that some intellectuals might go to the villages and use their entrepreneurship to create intellectual and political capital in the country side.

Deng's opposition to democracy and democratization was due to the fact that he did not quite trust the grassroots to be able to form a consensus around his economic reforms. But Deng also opposed the gerontocrats with patriarchal and bureaucratic mind set in the party and the government. Deng moved towards infusing young blood into the government and if he at all redistributed power then it was from the older to the younger members within the party.

There was yet another level in which Deng redistributed power; he attempted to give predominance to the State instead of the Party. The institutions connected to the State were impersonal, rational and more reliable and they followed the rule of law and respected contracts more than the party which relied on cronyism, networks and personal wills. It was here that Deng again sought the help of the intellectuals to help establish a rational-legal state in China. This returned in some manner the ideology of legalism, which was vehemently opposed in China. The Chinese had a dislike for legalism, counting the days of the cruel Shang in the Chinese prehistory and Deng insisted that unless the Party at the local levels was curbed, there could be no economic expansionism. Such moves by Deng bought widespread criticism among the people and he sought the help of the intellectuals to help create an acceptance for his programmes. This was in 1986 and only three years later, in 1989, Deng was to have them killed in the Tiananmen Square. However, while the romance with the intellectuals lasted they wrote pamphlets and campaigned against the conservatives of the Party and said that the old, unchanging juggernauts were opposing reforms. At that point of time, Deng never let his real intentions be known to any and which is that he merely used the intellectuals to flush out the conservative Communists but never really meant to have democracy[71].

Deng apprehended that allowing multi-party systems, contestations and conflicts, something which he felt would jeopardise his plans for high technology and capital intensive, urbanized and centralized growth promoted by international finance. The debate over democracy was not really over growth, but over whose growth; whether the growth would emanate out of the Pearl River Delta and Shanghai or whether the growth would be from the interior region of the Yellow River valley areas led by the town and village enterprise. The class struggle in China was not about labour versus capitalists

---

[71]"Chinese actions resulted from change in the world, the need to stifle dissent and maintain power for the Communist Party, from the growth of China's regional ambitions, and the very energy and unscrupulousness with which China pursued wealth and power." Richard Bernstein and Ross.H.Munro. The Coming Conflict With China. Vintage.USA. 1997. Pg 44.

or the village versus the city but it was between the small petty entrepreneurs and the large and centralized global finance and among those who liberalization could help and those who would be marginalized in the process[72].

If it is assumed that the poor and backward people want the state run enterprises while those with higher purchasing power would look towards liberalization, in China quite contrary has been the case. It has been the so-called losers of the Great Leap of Mao who wished for liberalization while the winners wanted the state to retain control over many enterprises. The possible reason for this was that the state enterprises helped a dual price structure in which those connected with the sale of goods produced by the State owned enterprises could make profits from resale of the products at a higher price in a parallel market. This hurt the less well-off badly and because the town and village enterprises could produce almost all the products which the State owned enterprises produced, they wanted the State Owned Enterprises to be scaled down and private capital in its place. Due to this dual economy, prices of every commodity rose and in the years 1986 and 1987, inflation sky rocketed bringing about a spate of student unrest across the country. Not to be discouraged by the failure of the economy, Deng liberalized prices but not production and prices rose further by another 20% over and above to what existed. China was an economic disaster waiting to happen. The dual track economy seemed to be the culprit.

With these failures on the prices, authoritarian voices

---

[72]Ibid. pg 45.

continued to find more space in the Party. Li Peng was already a contending Premier of China and Wu Jiaxing, a researcher in the party's research bureau in Beijing were now strong voices of neo authoritarianism. Clearly, the Party saw China's redemption in authoritarianism. They assigned China's crisis and its inflation to whatever decentralization Deng brought about. In a country like China where political power is automatically translated into economic power, Deng thought that higher political powers to the villages and provinces encouraged speculation and corruption. He assigned the crisis of prices to such locally shared and redistributed power. Deng now thought that the Party should once again be in command and the institutions of the State will be relegated back. Deng reversed his earlier decisions on the prominence of the State and once more restored the Party to power. This reversal in Deng's views on democracy had a lot to do with the massacre at the Tiananmen Square.

References:

1. Ezra. F.Vogel. Deng Xiaoping and the Transformation of China. Harvard University Press. USA. 2011.

2. Henry Kissinger. On China. Penguin. USA. 2010.

Chapter Nine

Deng's Industrialization, Regionalism, Taiwan and Hong Kong and Rest of the World

The fundamental premise of Deng's market economy was that if China was to become the epitome of socialism it had to first pass through capitalism and capitalism could develop only if the economy of China was opened up to market forces. The opening China to the market was not without its problems. The strong hold of local leaders of Communist party and the semi feudal relations of production made things difficult for the liberal forces of the market to take shape. Besides, China's industries were owned by the State, known as the State Owned Enterprises which ran on losses and these became a drag on the Chinese exchequer. The losses were so high and mounted at alarming rates that one could not get interested buyers. Nonetheless, Deng started his opening up of the economy through the disinvestment of the State Owned Enterprises, henceforth the SOEs. This would be the situation in 1979.

The stumbling block in the disinvestment of the SOEs came from the workers; the workers did not easily let go of their employment because disinvestments would indeed mean retrenchment. Deng co-opted the workers by turning the SOEs into cooperatives by which the workers became the owners of these units and hence instead of being against the management became the management. This form of ownership of companies by workers came to be known as the stock cooperatives. Next, Deng started creating sponsored conglomerates along the lines of the Korean Chaebols. In this way the stronger units were to agglomerate within them the weaker ones and hence averted the need to raise funds through expensive bank loans. The Korean Chaebols did not work well because they soon developed unholy nexus between banks and corrupt politicians. Deng was clear that strong workers' management would prevent such nexus. Deng also freed the SOE management from the party diktats so that they could take apt decisions to suit market conditions. In an economy where economics and politics are so closely related, Deng made sure that the workers were sufficiently empowered as voters as well as free to operate as owners of enterprises. Deng was already keen on extending democracy and power to the workers and the managers away from the affiliations of the party seemed to help the cause. Democracy, for Deng thus had an important economic function as well.

The idea of worker run enterprise was not so new in China because at least ten years before Deng's experiment, the peasants and workers who returned to the village as retrenched persons from SOEs took over the town and village enterprises known as the TVEs and started running them; if not to produce the things that were meant to be produced in them then at least use these factories as premises for running small businesses. Village councils also started investing in these TVEs and many farmers used their savings to revive such enterprises. Indeed, such TVEs were the sources of China's cheap assembled electronic products like calculators, televisions and computers that were to take the world over. The TVE's did not really thrive on their own and soon lost steam and lost out to investors from Hong Kong, Taiwan and even Macao. These outlying lands of erstwhile Imperial China yearned to be united to the mainland in a manner of nostalgia for motherland and investments were a method of seeking the larger unity[73].

Thus on the one hand, one part of Deng's reforms in the form of stock management cooperatives and management controlled SOEs complemented the other arm of reforms namely integrating China with its richer counterparts like Taiwan and Hong Kong. The Chinese who lived in these areas were homesick and nostalgic and yearned to return to the mainland one day; in fact the names of streets and squares in Taiwan were after the streams, hills and rivers of mainland China. In 1997, after the General Elections, the ruling regime of the Kuomintang suffered a setback and the new powers were eager to integrate at least economically with China. Just at this instance, migration of labour was already taking place in the Pearl River Delta and the investors from China grabbed this opportunity to become even more competitive by relocating their businesses in the mainland.

---

[73]Willem Van Kemenade. China, Hong Kong, Taiwan Inc. - The Dynamics of a New Empire. Vintage. New York. 1998. Pp 70-71.

Taiwan

On the strait of Formosa, Taiwan previously known as Formosa is a province of the mainland China with a President without being a sovereign country. The original inhabitants were of aboriginal stock that is related to the various Philippine groups and to the Dyaks of Borneo. The Chinese migrated from the mainland into Taiwan some three hundred years ago when the Chinese Emperor raided the place. Between 1895 and 1945, Taiwan was under Japanese occupation. But in 1949, when Chiang Kai Shek's nationalist party stormed into Taiwan and assumed control over the territory, the Communists from mainland China staked claims to Taiwan insisting that the territory had always belonged to China. Taiwan continued to be the "homeland" to Chiang Kai Shek's Koumintang and with the commencement of the Cold War, the USA wholly supported the Koumingtang as a base against the Communist nations of the Soviet Union and China. For Communist China, Taiwan's existence as an independent territory under the command of the nationalists was looked upon as an antonym of its own polity and ideology and repeatedly attacked the territory. The greater the threat was from China, the greater was the military fortification of Taiwan by the USA.

The Taiwanese felt helpless at the play of militarism over their territory and looked for peace. They neither wanted a US stooge in the Koumingtang nor were happy with attacks of the communists. Like Hong Kong, Taiwan too wanted autonomy to decide over its own affairs. Besides, Taiwan was occupied by the nationalist Chinese who constituted the elites of China. These Chinese of Taiwan were far more prosperous than the mainland brethren and it was natural that the Communists would not tolerate the capitalist model that delivered more economic prosperity than the Communist one.

Taiwan as a territory of the Koumingtang began with a liberal dose of American aid. Chiang Kai Shek built the highest dam in the world completing the project in record time. Forests were cut down recklessly to build roads, bridges, canals, industries and ports. Between 1951 and 1964, the industrial output of Taiwan rose by 300% and the regime was free of American aid. Central to this reckless pace of development, education perhaps got more than a fair share. The number of primary schools rose over 40% and that of secondary schools by over 70%. Independent colleges were set up under one University. But Taiwan did not stop at this; it started fortifying islands of Quemoy and Matsue by keeping a few strong garrisons here. China retaliated by building up air bases along the coasts of Fukien and Kwangtun provinces. Such fortifications by China led to a souring of its relationships with the Soviet Union, sank China into the useless pursuit of military might which eventually strained the resources so much that China plunged into food insecurity. It seems that the Soviet Union threatened China with dire economic consequences if it went ahead with its militarism in the South China Sea; China tried to retaliate with increasing its economic might manifold in order to become free of Soviet aid just as Taiwan had become free of American aid while multiplying its output threefold over. The mindless pursuit of output of goods finally led to the Great Famine which killed anywhere between 5 and 10 million persons.

China was jealous of Taiwanese prosperity; it was also fearful of the success of the capitalist-nationalist model of economic growth. Taiwan under Chiang Kai Shek always sustained the dream of conquering the mainland and such belligerence made the mainland only react with even more hostility. But after Chiang's death in 1975, Ching Kuo succeeded him. Interestingly, Ching in Taiwan and Deng who now succeeded Mao in mainland China were class fellows in the Sun Yat Sen University in Moscow. Ching was once arrested in Moscow by Stalin because the former continued to be a Trostykite despite orders from Stalin to the contrary. This move by Stalin was also a favour to Mao who was then persecuting the Taiwanese and Ching was a prime Taiwanese. Ching was later released when Taiwan and China joined hands against the Japanese aggression on China during the Second World War. Stalin used Ching's release to amend the Sino Soviet relations.

Ching Kuo was a socialist, a nationalist and a Confucianist. When he assumed leadership of Taiwan moved the country from a one party dictatorship to a political pluralism. Travel from Taiwan to mainland was permitted, martial law relaxed and forming of democratic political parties were allowed. The names of streets in Taiwan which were after rivers and hills of the mainland were now named after native Taiwanese and aborigines who lived in the island prior to the Chinese invasions. It appears that Ching Kuo was trying to develop an indigenous Taiwanese identity as distinct from that of mainland China. Ching made the first move towards creating a distinct Taiwanese nation by developing a Taiwanese sense of identity and a Taiwanese nationalism to counter the hegemony of the Koumingtang. When Ching died in 1988 and Lee Teng Hui took over as the Premier, the process of weeding out the Koumingtang hegemony was accelerated. The free air which swept over Taiwan helped the country to grow economically by opening up the way for investors from all over the world especially from Japan. The development of Taiwanese nationalism also resisted any attempt by China to seek reunion with Taiwan.

US which has been a natural ally of Taiwan, recognising the country as the Republic of China as opposed to mainland China which it called the People's Republic of China started reversing its stand in 1972. In that year, the American President Richard Nixon visited mainland China and the Senate enacted the Taiwan Relations Act, or the TRA which stated that the US for all purposes of diplomacy and foreign relations will deal with Taiwan as a sovereign nation. While closeness to the mainland distanced Taiwan from the USA but the semantics of the TRA enthused a new sense of sovereignty among its people. When after the Tiananmen massacre in 1989 the Western nation boycotted China, Taiwanese merchants rushed to fill in the gap. Investments flowed from Taiwan into China. China started producing those goods which Taiwan would make.

Taiwan and China relations developed around two loops. On one loop, China was eager to maintain good relations with Taiwan in order to prevent the latter from shifting investments away from China to Vietnam and the Philippines while on the other hand, Taiwan used its economic might over China to retain its political sovereignty. For China, Taiwan's political sovereignty is a threat because Taiwan is leveraged by Japan and the Western powers against China. Yet, Taiwan and China are close to each other; every youth in Taiwan hopes to return to the mainland home someday and every mainland Chinese hopes to be able to call Taiwan as an integral part of its home. For the Taiwan Chinese, Taiwan is an exile and for the Chinese on the mainland, it is a wait for the Taiwanese to return home. This spirit of oneness that an age old civilization has given is repeatedly challenged by the contemporaneity of Communism and the resistance towards it.

Since 2004, another dimension was added to the entire politics around the South China Sea. China started buying up half of the world's natural resources like iron ore, nickel, copper, silver, zinc and others. These were the same raw materials which Japan also needed and in the past have invaded both Russia and China for gaining access to these mineral resources. Taiwan becomes very crucial in the entire story of minerals. China wants to control the South China Sea because of its trade in mineral resources while Japan uses Taiwan to maintain its presence in the sea. China and Taiwan are thus equally balanced in the tug of war over political sovereignty.

Despite such liberalizations, Deng never agreed to full capital account convertibility with Taiwan. There was a strong pressure to do this especially because China had very high levels of savings, low debts and huge reserves in the banks;

money was cheap. Therefore, Deng ensured that the Chinese savings did not flow out to Taiwan to swell hedge funds and other speculative businesses. In the aftermath of the Asian financial meltdown US funds flowed out of Hong Kong plummeting its exports and the GDP, Chinese funds held in reserves of huge savings flowed into this territory for investing in infrastructure and public goods and constructions and thus helped tide over the crisis.

By 2009, China was already directing substantial investments into Taiwan. China signed a deal of £3.8 billion with Taiwan in which the Chinese electronics companies like Lenovo, Haier, Sino Steel and others were to buy back from the Taiwanese, liquid crystal display panels and memory chips. Air traffic opened between the two countries and soon the Chinese were allowed to invest over one hundred different sectors in Taiwan. The more prominent sectors included textiles, iron and steel, telecommunication, and real estate, hotel, tourism and airport management. Soon Taiwanese companies were exporting millions of dollars' worth flat screen TV sets to China. Naturally when the US started supplying arms to Taiwan, China was furious with the US but not with Taiwan[74]. Eric Weiner (2009) writes that Investing into Taiwan, opening up markets, reducing tariffs and liberalising trade was part of China's grand plan of eventually gobbling up Taiwan[75]. Interestingly, China invested into Taiwan industries to help Taiwan attain a

---

[74]Eric.J.Weiner. The Shadow Market. How Sovereign Wealth Funds Secretly Dominate the Global Economy. Oneworld. USA. 2011.
[75]Ibid

trade surplus with China in the commodities sector while China accumulated surpluses through the export of services. Investments of China into Taiwan did not take place through private investments but through the sovereign wealth fund with the Chinese government.

Inside Mainland China

Deng's industrial policy was aimed at the rapid development of the Pearl River Delta region where Hong Kong and Macao had already become an industrial hub. Guangdong, Guangzhou, Zhuhai and Shenzhen were to join Hong Kong and Macau as a swathe of rich and fertile hinterland. Traditionally these provinces constituted those parts of China that were treated as being peripheral to mainland earmarked only for the sea coast trade conducted between Chinese traders and foreigners over various eras of history. Deng decided to absorb these outlying areas of China, marginal to its economy and peripheral to its society into the economic zone earmarked for high and exemplary growth. In a period of ten years the sleepy fishing villages had emerged as leading economic zones of China and there grew in Beijing a new found respect for the blue areas as being superior to the yellow interior.

Traditionally, the provinces of Guangdong and Guangzhou were treated as southern expanses of the Chinese empire; home to the Baiyeu people also known as the Zhuang who spoke a different language. These provinces were treated more like buffer zones to weather attacks to China across the seas. Generally forsaken by the mainland Chinese, these areas were not reckoned with as being cultured and developed. During the Opium War, these provinces were the centres of trade, the location of anti-Machu demonstrations and of Taipei Rebellion. In Communist China, these provinces were purposely neglected since Mao considered them as being vulnerable to American naval offensive. Expectedly these provinces were left poor, unaided and not integrated to the overall Chinese economic systems. But Deng changed all that and focussed his energies on these hitherto neglected provinces. In fact, with the opening up of the Chinese economy, Guangdong and the port province of Fujian received so much of financial investments that they no longer had the need to have any aid from Beijing. These provinces had their own finances.

Guangdong and Fujian were given SEZ statuses with exemptions from import duties and easy bank loans. These regions became such large exchange earners that they contributed liberally to the State exchequer while retaining the bulk of the revenues for their own purposes of investments and administration. The real estate prices in these provinces escalated so much that the relative prices of property in Shanghai fell. The Shanghai lobby was annoyed with Beijing and clamoured to put brakes on the Pearl River Delta provinces. Deng himself saw a sense in this demand especially because Guangdong, Fujian, Guangzhou and other Pearl River Delta provinces were becoming close to Hong Kong and Taiwan and through that to the Western powers and/or to South Korea and Japan. Hence Beijing developed several macroeconomic and policy interventions to reign in and curb

Guangdong.

Among the policies redesigned for the Pearl River Delta provinces and SEZ was curb on liberal bank loans, curbs on speculative investments in the real estate sectors and raise in the portion of revenues to be made over to the central exchequer. These were designed to let Shanghai over take the Guangdong province and also, according to some experts redistribute revenues from these prosperous provinces to the poorer provinces. But in the end, it was observed that the surpluses from Guangdong were taken out to develop Shanghai's super city zone Pudong into a massive real estate hub while the poorer interior provinces got nothing. As expected, dissatisfaction and protests followed.

In order to manage such open favouritism towards Shanghai and disfavour towards the poorer interior, China now developed yet another policy of locating heavy industries with sophisticated technology off the coastal areas, known as the blue zones, blue in order to signify the ocean. The labour intensive industries were located in the interior and less urbanized areas also known as the yellow zone, yellow to signify the alluvial deposits from the Yangstze Kiang River Valley. While this did appease the interior provinces somewhat, also because they felt their human resources better used in labour intensive industries and also somewhat more integral to their way of circulating social capital, the conflict between Shanghai and Guangdong continued over what kind of heavy industries each would get. Shanghai won again because industries with scientific sophistication were located here.

Chinese scholars have often asked why is it that Deng favoured Shanghai especially the Pudong area in his scheme of things in the 1990's when in the 1980's it appeared that Deng was keen on the Pearl River Delta. Shanghai has always been a centre of culture and cosmopolitanism. In 1928, the city had Jews, Japanese, Europeans and Russians. The people, both Chinese as well as the foreigners made many fortunes in the city. In a struggle for control between Chiang Kai Shek's Koumingtan and Mao's Communists, the latter took control over Shanghai. Given the residence of the super-rich and educated and urbanized people here, Mao located heavy industries in this region. Housing was developed mainly to host the numerous workers in this city. It appears that while Shanghai contributed generous amounts of taxes to the central exchequer, it hardly received any investments in return; a Shanghainese who returned to the city after forty years said that the city had not even been cleaned all the while that he lived away from it.

Interestingly Shanghai hosted a large number of state owned enterprises but also a fanatic left in the days of the Cultural Revolution. After the death of Mao and the elimination of the Gang of Four, Deng decided to punish China for its weakness for the Maoist culture. Shanghai was deprived of benefits from the exchequer. But soon there was a change in the policy; Shanghai returned to Beijing's favour in the late 1990's. The move to develop Shanghai ahead of the Pearl River Delta was to now pull in the economic development of the coast into the mainland and Shanghai was to be the first post in the inner domain.

Deng developed Shanghai first by relaxing the taxes that the city had to pay to the Central Exchequer. He then made credit rules easy, issued debt bonds, leased lands for the development of SEZ and real estate. Despite these efforts, Shanghai's GDP grew annually at no more than 5% when for the rest of China it was 9%. This was in the 1980's. But in the 1990's Deng created Shanghai on the model of the Pearl River Delta and Hong Kong with super markets, large departmental stores, foreign investments, various tax cuts and exemptions, liberal land leases. Shanghai grew at an astronomical pace; it was China's own Hong Kong. In Shanghai, Deng tried to show as if China like Hong Kong and Taiwan has been able to perform similar fetes.

Shanghai had been an old city but Pudong, the new suburb of the city now became the new business centre with IT Parks, export processing zones, banking, investments, and commodity exchanges, new aerodrome and port, and it became the Manhattan of the east. Interestingly, while Mao focussed on industries for Shanghai and all through the 1980's Deng thought of exports based out of Shanghai, in the 1990's the policy for Shanghai was to develop it similar to the service oriented economies of Hong Kong. The idea of a liberal and market driven economy in the 1980's was export competitiveness and export orientation, but by the end of the 1990's, economic liberalisation meant being host to global financial flows, speculative futures, commodity exchange and swaps. This meant a deeper integration between China and Hong Kong and Shanghai became China's own Hong Kong. In order to be able to do this there was a need to show to the world that China is now ready with its own version of Hong Kong, namely Shanghai and the Pearl River Delta was now relegated in importance since China largely dispensed with Hong Kong.

Though the Shanghai Stock Exchange developed the market was dualistic. There was an A market for the domestic players and a B market for foreigners. The B market was limited but the A market was a haven of insider traders, scamsters and other kinds of shady dealers. Millions of peasants and workers, retired professors, housewives, out of job persons lost money on the Shanghai Stock Exchange. The media and the newspapers always portrayed rosy images of the share market and lured people to buy more and more till in 1993 the crash of Shanghai market became the largest share market scandal of the country. It was not until much later after Deng's death in 1997 that Shanghai slowly found its feet and reputation. The speed and urgency with which Deng developed Shanghai was also due to the transfer of Hong Kong to China in 1997. There was no way in which Hong Kong once transferred into China would be allowed to retain its superiority over the Chinese mainland and Shanghai had to come up to and even surpass Hong Kong's superiority when the time came for the latter's integration into the People's Republic of China.

Hong Kong

Hong Kong along with Macau is the two Special Administrative Regions of SARs of China. This means that though these regions are contained within the nation and state called China, they have their own systems of law and administration. Hong Kong had passed under British control ever since the first Opium War 1832 to 1842 except for a brief interlude of Japanese occupation and control during Pacific War in 1941 but was soon transferred under British administration till 1997. While a section of Chinese proletariat migrated to Hong Kong from the coastal regions of southern China, but a large number of very rich and sophisticated merchants from Shanghai and Guangdong also found their haven in Hong Kong. During the Cold War when China was isolated by the Western world, Hong Kong rose to prominence through the investments and acumen of the Shanghai business class. Adequate infrastructure, good governance, easy laws, liberal governance of the British helped these business persons to make a mark in business. Soon investments started flowing into Hong Kong from the Western world where high wages made business non conducive to competitiveness. Japan invested heavily in Korea treating the country almost as an extended economic territory, and Western Europe, probably to contain Japan invested similarly in Hong Kong. Much of China's prosperity today lies in investments from Hong Kong finding its way back into China southern provinces.

In order to understand Hong Kong one must understand the importance of Shanghai in the society and economy of China. Shanghai has been the haven of trade, finance, investments since pre modern days in China. Shanghai is the leading cultural city of China. Historically, southern China has been economically and culturally more developed than the rest of the country and this is because it was relatively safe from attacks from nomadic territories that bordered China on the north and the west. The city of Changa'n where the Silk Road terminated and its trade culminated appears to be a forerunner of Shanghai in influence. Shanghai was especially prominent during the Qing dynasty flourishing with trade with the Western powers especially the British East India Company. Many merchants made money with the opium trade and later during the Nationalist Movement also financed China's Chiang Kai Shek's army. Mao flushed out these merchants who he felt would become a counter force to his own Communist movement. Many such merchants fled to Taiwan and Hong Kong. Interestingly, when during the Korean War in 1950 the Communist North Korea attacked the liberal South Korea and the US placed its Seventh Fleet in Taiwan and blocked the entire South China Sea, Hong Kong was the port through which supplies continued to be made into the mainland China. Interestingly, this trade enriched many of the Hong Kong merchants and in many ways the Korean War started up a new chapter of prosperity in the island state.

While the British did not openly oppose the US in its containment of China, yet Britain made it clear that it was not in the game. China amply rewarded Britain for this and allowed access of Hong Kong merchants to access opportunities in the mainland. By the end of the 1960's the violence of the Cultural Revolution forced streams of refugees from the mainland to flee into Hong Kong. In 1970 over half of the population of Hong Kong consisted of refugees from the mainland. This population served the cheap labour upon which the various industries of Hong Kong flourished. Television, computers, washing machines, automobiles and a variety of assembled goods where prices of goods produced from Hong Kong were substantially lower than in the rest of the world.

The flourish of Hong Kong appeared to suffer when after the opening up of China to the market economy took place in the middle of the 1980's with the coming of Deng Xiaoping. Entrepreneurs from Hong Kong made a rush back to the mainland of China, albeit in the southern provinces. The migration from Hong Kong to the mainland was so strong that the British government of Hong Kong began to worry and relations between Britain and China suffered. China however created a nationalist hysteria among the Hong Kong Chinese making them to believe that the Chinese economy is to increase manifold with the economic reforms. During this time, the Western media, credit rating agencies and other analysts opined that since the Chinese State owned enterprises, or the SOEs had huge accumulated losses and were in no position to expand production frontiers to cater for a market driven economy. Deng allowed a free flow of foreign investments into China in a bid to industrialize the same. One of Deng's purposes in opening up the economy to foreign trade was also to allow the investors from Hong Kong invest freely in China. It was the combined work of various factors which embittered relationships between China and Hong Kong. The emigration of Hong Kong Chinese into mainland, partly out of homesickness and partly due to expanded opportunities in the mainland and the global recession which hit Great Britain's economy and the decline of investments in Hong Kong because of many entrepreneurs returned to China, relations between the two nations, namely Britain and China soured.

Interestingly in the 1990's, just about seven years away from the lapse of control over Hong Kong the British invested heavily in the country. Britain built a $ 20 million new super airport complex namely the Chek Lap Kok. One wonders why Britain invested so heavily in a colony that they were about to relinquish but the airport complex was at the centre of the new arrangement that Hong Kong was to have. The provisions of Special Administrative Area were designed in a manner so as to be able to protect Britain's investments in Hong Kong. Besides, British wanted China to be really jealous of all the investments that Hong Kong was getting, something that China desired for itself. One of the ways was to allow democracy in Hong Kong so that the Legislative Council would have more power than the Executive Council and this would have protected British investments better in Hong Kong. Much of the West's insistence that democracy comes to China is tied to their interests in protecting their investments; democracy provides voice to the Legislators and prevents authoritarianism from dictating arbitrary policies. China, on the other hand has never been comfortable with democracy because of its autocratic manner of centralized decision making.

China read Britain's recipes for the transfer of power as being one in which the Western powers would continue to keep their hold over Chinese affairs through Hong Kong. In 1997, China threatened to withdraw all financial support from the airport project if Britain laid too many conditions on the administrative format of the SAR for Hong Kong. Britain, not to be threatened by China said that they would get the entire Western world to rally investments into Hong Kong; China toed the British line for fear of losing its status as the prime investor into Hong Kong. China had financed the gigantic investment project from its trade surpluses by exporting cheap goods to everywhere in the world. Were the western investors to return to Hong Kong, then the Hong Kong investors who had migrated to mainland China might return back to Hong Kong? China was very eager to maintain its dominance in the world economy and for this purpose it was important that it retained its hold over investments in Hong Kong.

Just as Britain campaigned for democracy in Hong Kong in order to be able to maintain a hold over the country's political processes and hence be able to guard its economic interests, China invoked strong nationalist feelings among the Hong Kong Chinese in order to have a political influence over a people in order to be able to access its economic interests.

South Korea

China's relationship with a democratic South Korea is fraught with hesitation and doubt, because the Communist North Korea is China's natural ally. While North Korea is 82nd on the list of Chinese trade partners, China is the largest trade partner for North Korea. Trade and security issues, especially of nuclear weapons facilities make North Korea into an important ally for China. However, economic ties with South Korea appeared to be more lucrative as China started opening up its economy. The economic exchanges were paltry and halting till the 1997 meltdown in the Tiger economies, which include Thailand, Singapore, Taiwan and South Korea. After the meltdown, global investors withdrew their money from these economies and naturally a much liberalized China was the preferred host for these investments. Many Korean companies especially Daewoo, Hyundai, Samsung and LG were now investing in China to cater to its large population, growing middle class and the growing cities. The relocation of these industries actually led to a growth in Korean investments in China in its numerous small firms which were ancillaries to these large manufacturers of consumer durables.

South Korea investments into China have actually led to a further rise in the competitiveness of the Chinese products, especially in the manufacture of electronic drives, TV sets, computers, stainless steel and many sophisticated metal products that are needed in the manufacture of value-added consumer products. The trade accounts are settled in the Chinese currencies and thus Chinese imports from Korea makes way for further deployment of Chinese money into the bulk of Korean industries, namely ship building and defence equipments. What is even interesting is that the Chinese money held in Korea through trade surpluses was now invested in hi tech Korean firms in the energy and IT sector. The insistence of China in retaining its currency in the Korean market actually helped China take control over the

Korean economy.

Vietnam

China had a sour relation with Vietnam ever since it attacked Vietnam in 1979. However, the Vietnam government, albeit much to the distress of its people sought Chinese investments especially in its steel sector. Vietnam accumulated a large trade surplus with China, which China used to reinvest in acquiring natural resources assets, especially bauxite of which Vietnam is the third largest producer in the world.

South East Asia Infrastructure Fund

China holds a fund, mainly funded by the government called the South east Asia Infrastructure Fund, which funds various projects and also supports the currencies like the baht in lieu of both minerals and markets.

Australia

Around 2005, Australian giants namely Rio Tinto and BHP Billiton became even larger by exporting iron ore to China. While China has the world's largest reserves of iron ore, yet the needs of its ever growing steelmaking capacity seemed to need every tonne of iron ore that was in the world. In view of this, China became a very large market for iron ore. However, as the Chinese demand dropped off leading to a worldwide collapse of iron ore prices, and along with the growing restrictions on mining from the

Australian government, margins in the business were getting pressed. Rio Tinto and BHP Billiton were eager to exit from mining. Chinese companies, especially China's SOE, Min Metals bought many such mines and thus expanded China's command over resources. In fact a consortium of Chinese power producing companies have entered into a £40 million with Australian coal mines. SinoSteel Company of China bought the iron ore company called Midwest and the two large aluminium producing companies called Chinalco and Alcoa bought a 12% stake in Rio Tinto.

Latin America

In a similar vein, China invested in Jamaica and Argentina to procure large natural resources assets. Jamaica always looks towards the US or the EU to bail out its economy. However by 2009, the conditions of US and EU were so fragile that the Jamaican government looked towards China for relief. China eagerly stepped and wanted bauxite reserves in the country. Jamaica is the world's fourth largest bauxite producer. In case of Argentina, China gave the much needed support to jack up the peso; Argentina is important for China because it supplies two third of China's need for soya beans. Argentina also looked towards the Chinese wealth funds in order to bail out its failing banks. Weiner writes that when Argentina feared that the peso was losing steam, the Chinese would step in with their money that would be construed as a future payment for soya beans, of which China is one of the largest buyers. Recently in 2013, China has stepped up its activities in Brazil setting up manufacturing units in order to process raw materials which today China owns through a similar instrument of currency swaps. Chinese wealth is fuelling Brazil's manufacturing sector especially steel through active currency swaps between the two countries[76].

China's Pattern of Investments:

China globalizes in rather interesting ways; it lends money to nations in need such as Greece, Argentina, Jamaica and others. It often uses the trade surpluses from a country to invest in those industries that would export goods back to China and hence gain control over the sector that export to China as in South Korea, Vietnam and India. The third instrument China uses is to buy up debt funds and engage in currency swaps as between Argentina and China or Brazil and China. China lends to Greece when the latter is in need of money and Greece is the gateway to the Balkans. China is buying up stakes in the privatization of the railways in the Balkans[77]. China is investing heavily in Ireland in infrastructure related projects, real estate and the building of shopping malls, schools, manufacturing units and railways. In Spain, China is funding tourism and via Brazil helping Spain to wind up its properties in Brazil, an erstwhile Spanish colony.

If China is a net importer from countries like South Korea and Japan, China sees to it that the trade surpluses which the

---

[76]Bloomberg, 26th March 2011. Internet sources.

[77]POSRI. Summer Vol 3. 2011

partner countries earn are spend in such a manner so as to increase the Chinese control over those sectors of the economy. Surpluses out of trade with China, which are accumulated in Japan are invested in the Japanese stock markets and IT companies. Similarly it is with South Korea where China invests in those very firms that export to China. The Chinese are found on both sides of trade; they double up as both the importer as well as the exporter. The Indian case is very interesting; China exports coal to India, with the money which it earns out of coal are invested in purchasing iron ore; the profits that the iron ore suppliers make are once more directed for investments in steel units or pellet plants from which again the Chinese buy. China can do this because it insists in settling accounts in the Chinese currency, which gives the Chinese clearing houses power over reinvesting decisions.

The Chinese invest in companies that explore natural resources. In China, wealth is not held with the private individuals nor with the State Owned Enterprises; the government own most wealth. These funds are used to spread China's control over the various economies of the world. Sovereign funds are channelized through the SOEs. Instances of such investments are Sinopec's £4.4 billion to buy Addax Petroleum, a Swiss oil exploration company having reserves in Nigeria, Gabon and Iraq. China National Offshore Oil Corporation, CNOOC purchased the Norweigian oil servicing firm, AWILCO Offshore at £1.25 billion. Similarly, Chinese invest in European and American firms that have reserves across the world.

The Chinese demand raises prices of every mineral in

the world and China uses these trade deficits once again by reinvesting them in deepening its hold over mineral assets. Suppose, China spends money to buy oil from Nigeria, it will see to it that the money that Nigeria earns is spent on expanding the hold of the exporting company in which China has already bought its stakes. China's games are well planned and are very long term. The directions of Chinese investments are really not the control over markets, but control over natural resources and ocean and land routes. Dambisa Moyo (2012)[78] observes that China has put all of us into a race over the various natural resources through its unprecedented appetite for raw materials, food and fuel. China is looking towards water resources in north east India and Tibet, coal in Iran, shale gas in Bahrain, arable land in Africa, gold and silver in South Africa and has bought an entire mountain in Peru that makes China the owner of the world's largest copper deposits.

Moyo[79] raises an important question and which is that China is itself well-endowed with minerals and raw materials so why does it really need so much of resources from countries abroad? A possible reason that Moyo suggests is perhaps because China wants to control global economies and global productions and hence it is not content with what it merely has; it is looking towards countries like Mozambique and Malawi, Colombia and Cameroons, Bolivia and Brazil, Kazakhstan and Kenya, lands that no one regards, lands that no one notices and uses these to build up edifices of not only

---

[78]Dambisa Moyo. Winner Take All -China's Race For Resources and What It Means For Us. Penguin. USA. 2012.
[79]Ibid. pg 96.

raw material trading and excavation but of setting up value added industries and building up economies based upon higher value addition than just what mineral trade would enable. China has a plan for the world at large and the Chinese strategies cannot only be understood as the enhancement of nationalism.

References:

1. Barry Naughton. The Chinese Economy – Transitions and Growth. The MIT Press. Massachusetts and London. 2006.

2. Richard Bernstein and Ross.H.Munro. The Coming Conflict With China. Vintage Books. London. 1998.

3. Willem Van Kemenade. China, Hong Kong, Taiwan Inc – The Dynamics of a New Empire. Vintage. New York. 1998.

4. Dambisa Moyo. Winner Take All – China's Race For Resources and what It Means For Us. Penguin. USA. 2012.

Chapter Ten

US and China

China's growth will have an important consequence for the United States which commands the global politics as a monopoly of force after the demise of the Soviet Union. United States is likely to regard China's growth as a political threat to the region and to the world at large. The United States was drawn into the Chinese affair at first when it supported the European powers against the Qing dynasty and then later as it tried to contain in Japan's rapacious loot of China's mineral resources especially in the inter war period. The United States stepped into the Chinese affair with more determination when the Cold War broke out in the aftermath of the WWII and USA and the Soviet Union looked for mutually balancing each other's powers. China looks at the USA not so much as a competitor in its desire for world domination, but an essential force that needs to be held in balance so that every other kind of contingencies are taken care of and China is free to pursue its dreams ceteris paribus.

Between 1911 and 1949, China was divided internally between the Nationalists and the Communists. Soviet Union ideologically supported the Communists but favoured the Nationalists for two reasons. The presence of the Nationalists would ensure Soviet Union's access to China's mineral resources in Inner Mongolia and the Hunan areas as well as access to ports like Lushun while Communists might not concede to the Soviet demands easily. Japan, Soviet Union's enemy was also interested in the same areas as the latter was for the purpose of access of mineral wealth. Japan has the world's largest steel industry after China and for a long time has remained the largest producer of steel and yet it neither has iron ore nor coal. China provides for both these minerals to Japan apart from India. The interest in mineral properties makes both Japan and Soviet Union into natural enemies over China. The United States which has investments to protect in Taiwan, Hong Kong and Japan is a keen protector of Japanese interests and after the Cold War has the Soviet Union as its natural enemy. China therefore is a theatre for global détente. China's huge demographic might and the sheer size of the country were thought to hold the powers of Soviet Union, United States and Japan in balance.

Henry Kissinger analyses China in terms of its ancient philosophy and reveals that China is not keen to emerge out of the situation; instead it wants to maintain a balance among powers and hence playing one against the other to keep everyone distracted and thus divert attention from itself is a way of the Chinese military strategy. China may not go for total victory at war; but might just maintain everyone else in their mutual positions. Interestingly, Lee Kuan Yee, the Singapore leader too thinks in this way; for him China is the balance rather than it being a cog in the balancing wheel. China, he says is more likely to be interested in peace than in war[80].

But where the Sino-US balance might tip in favour of China is in the latter's accumulation of huge trade surpluses with the US. In 2013, China has a 0.3 trillion US dollars' worth trade surplus with the USA[81]. In fact, much like the situation precipitating the Opium war, the US has everything to buy from China, whether it is Chinese imitation of its best brands or whether it is from American firms outsourced in China. China is using the trade balance to buy up debt instruments, something the US may not tolerate too far. War might turn the situation in favour of the US, where Japan and Korea might emerge to play vital roles in view of excellent defence equipment manufacturing industries they have. Fear of war may reign in China but economic compulsions are strong too. China might like to "invest" the earnings from US exports elsewhere and thus build up aggressions around Tibet and India, relatively softer targets. China is not too keen to really attack the USA militarily; instead it is keener to cultivate the country as a friend and eventually to be able to influence its fiscal policy using to its advantage the large trade surpluses. China has used the trade surpluses to buy off US debt instruments and a large scale sale of such instruments might crash the dollar leading to the US's miseries for that would weaken its situation even more vis-à-vis the Chinese currency[82].

---

[80]Lee Kuan Yew - The Grand Master's Insights on China, United States and the World. Belfer Centre Studies in International Security. USA. 2013.Pp38-39

[81]United States Census; Foreign Trade, 2014.

[82]Eric. J. Weiner. The Shadow Market - How Sovereign Wealth Funds Secretly Dominate The Global Economy. Oneworld. UK. 2011. Pp 78-79.

The US has always found it difficult to determine the extent of Chinese trade surplus vis-à-vis her own. The statistics differ violently. Nearly 60% of Chinese exports to the USA are actually exports from Hong Kong and Singapore counted as being exported from China. Moreover, countries like South Korea, Singapore and Taiwan have invested huge amounts of money in China, which have boosted trade surpluses. China appears to have flagrantly violated copyrights and patents as every brand is locally produced in the country, copied like to like. Video games, books, white goods, electronic items, clothes, perfumes, cosmetics and automobiles of every brand on earth is flagrantly produced locally in China. USA has often made frantic pleas to close down such factories in China but unfortunately to no avail. Indeed, the growing trade deficit with China of the USA and the huge quantities of US debt instruments that China holds is increasingly making the US economy vulnerable to the Chinese exports.

The USA is in the throes of a recession since 2008; it is important for the USA to recover fast in order for it not to see redemption through war. War would be dangerous to both the USA and China, the two of the world's largest economies. Lee Kuan Yew thinks that the USA may take on upon itself the role that China had for so long prior to its awakening into this economic miracle. USA, like China of the Mao era, looks upon itself as the balance between India, Japan and Russia, a counterpoint to China and its tentacles in the countries around the South China Sea and the Indian Ocean. It is becoming more and more clear that the USA cannot pare China; it has to grow bigger and bigger if it has to keep China in check. China is moving rather rapidly along the Pacific Rim as well with active trade and investments with Japan and South Korea; where China cannot fire from the barrel of a gun, it will do so through the keel of merchant navy[83].

China has been always wary of the US. Indeed in 1997 when the time came for the transfer of sovereignty of Hong Kong to China from Great Britain, China openly called the move as a well-orchestrated Cold War with Hong Kong as the pawn. Ever since Mao, China had wanted to be as powerful as the Soviet Union and the statement of 1997 seemed to be a vindication of China's superiority in the world theatre. China took all the classical steps of the Cold War; it refused to contain in its arms built up, cancelled a subway system contract with France and a nuclear power plant that was to come up in the southern province of Guangdong. Holland and Germany were asked to forego further arms deals with Taiwan. US for the time being resisted granting the MFN status to China. The USA has harped on Taiwan and Tibet, one beyond the control of China and the other forcefully dominated by China. Things were cleared later as China offered many contracts for large projects and offered avenues for outsourcing and investments in its territory to Holland, France and Germany. In all these, we sense China's attempt to divide and rule the Western world and especially to isolate the USA.

The isolation of the USA in its economic affairs and granting special privileges to UK, France, Germany and Holland, China could manipulate the UN provisions just as it had done for the WTO while violating copy right laws. China

---

[83]Martin Jacques, Op cit 17. Pp 42-45.

defied every appeal to correct its human rights records and instead coordinated the Bangkok Declaration where many Asian countries clearly emphasized the right of every country to follow its own codes and not be dictated by western universals. The Bangkok declaration showed the solidarity of countries around the South China Sea on the grounds of a common Confucian culture. Samuel Huntington in his work, *Clash of Civilizations* opine that China convenes a cultural solidarity among those countries with similar cultures as its own and then extend a hand to the Islamic Bloc, its largest trading partner during the days of the Silk Road and together may pose a threat to the Western world[84].

Apropos to its cheap goods and local versions of global brands, China has also done enormously well in the production of arms and military weaponry. Today, countries like Israel, India, Pakistan, Sri Lanka and Myanmar and also Saudi Arabia have presented their shopping lists for missiles, and other weapons to China. China's military budget appears to have increased progressively as many of the erstwhile members of the PLA have invested in arms factories. Along with aviation, shipping, hotels and real estate, arms manufacture in China is a legitimate avenue of investment. Given the poor record of China in human rights, one of the quick sources of state revenue is a brisk trade in organs of executed criminals in the country.

According to the Chinese sources, Deng also never agreed to depreciation of the Chinese currency and in fact pegged the

---

[84]Samuel Huntington. Clash of Civilizations and the Remaking of the World Order. Penguin. USA. 1996

Chinese Renminbi to the US dollar. According to the American sources, China constantly intervened in the domestic market to keep the value of its currency low vis-à-vis the dollar so that it could penetrate the US markets and accumulate very large trade surpluses. The Americans say that China accumulated very large trade surpluses by selling cheap and with that surplus bought US treasury bonds. China is the largest creditor to the US today and holds the latter at ransom because at any point of time, China can crash the US economy.

If China had pegged its currency then this pegging the renminbi may have cost China its export markets especially in the face of newer competitors like India, yet China held steadfastly to its principles. Such a policy in fact helped China to emerge in a higher end market in the West and abandon the lower end market to newly emerging contenders of south Asia. By not devaluing currency, China may have lost its textile and steel market, or its plastics and chemicals market but it gained enormously in areas where it had hardly any competitors like arms, defence equipment, nuclear power equipment, steel making equipment and other such goods of sophisticated technology. The large bank balance that China held in the American banks and in the form of owning US treasury bonds basically came from supply of defence equipment, power equipment, real estate loans to the USA.

References:

1. Richard Bernstein and Ross.H.Munro. The Coming Conflict With China. Vintage Press. New York. 1998.

Chapter Eleven

China: An Investor's Point of View

Even though the base of the Chinese economy was created in its agriculture and in its local and small scale enterprises and in its "billion entrepreneurs", much of China's presence as a global power emanated out of the sectors where FDI was invested. Koneda Doggett and Subramanian, (2005)[85] have observed that there have been four stages of FDI in China. In Stage I, foreign firms located their factories in the Pearl River Delta region to take advantage of cheap labour from China. The manufactured goods of these firms would usually be exported. In Stage II, some of the low end spares and components were manufactured within China and infrastructure was locally developed to host these units. In Stage III, all inputs to assembly plants were made locally in China to be assembled by the foreign firms. In Stage IV, Chinese used the FDI as the invested money to manufacture goods themselves for the global market.

Ever since the days of liberalization, China decided to make exports and science and technology the pillars of its growth. This strategy in turn was based upon developing the

---

[85]Koneda Doggett and Subramanian, "Advantage China", Frontline, 25th March, 2005

agriculture and industry linkage. The linking of agriculture and industry, in which agriculture continued to produce cheap food for the non-food growing population and helped set up small and medium industries almost in a continuum from the village to the industry had actually helped fuel the engine of China's economic growth.   In 2008 with the hosting of the Olympics and in 2010 with the hosting of the World Trade Fair, China showcased its new found economic strength.   However, these "shows" also helped China's city based large industries especially the State owned enterprises to overcome their inertia and emerge as veritable economic powers. Billions of dollars were invested in building infrastructure which stimulated the setting up of numerous large and small steel making and fabrication units bringing in investments from private people and local bodies of the provincial administration, setting in motion numerous traders of metals and minerals, setting about the process of mining, electricity generation, and other activities.   These events showcased for the world set to spin many wheels of economic activity and the Chinese system rolled on. The State owned enterprises got a new lease of life as they supplied the essential raw materials for the infrastructure and other utilities for these events. The gargantuan scale of constructions required steady flow of workers from the villages and hence many restrictions had to be removed on migration and free movement of people. This not only raised the levels of urbanization from the 40% of the population in 2008 to the present rate of 52% but helped integrate the rural economy with that of the cities.

FDI in manufacturing helped China to develop a series

of linkages; both forward and backward. There were two levels of integration; one between design and industry and the other between supply and demand. The former value chain helped develop a strong service sector as in assembly and repairing services. The core industry that developed in China was that of the semiconductor industry; semiconductor industry had the deepest linkages with the local economy as it helped China to manufacture cheap inputs for a wide range of consumer industries, electronics, toys, cell phones and other gadgets. The import substitution efforts of the local industries in China were so successful that they cut down the import of semi-conductors by as much as 80%. China called this effort as one in which the country helped retain the valuable foreign exchange. As a backup to the semiconductor industry, China also set up the services like 3G, Wireless LAN (WAPI), DVD (EVD) and the RED DRAGON operating systems. The software and the hardware were now in place and China was the perfect host for outsourced units of Volkswagen of Germany, Hewlett Packard of the US, Sony and Toshiba from Japan all of who were now comfortably ensconced in the country.

Whenever we look at the Chinese growth story we are impressed with its linkages both backward and forward. Many global investors look at China's strength in the following ways:

1. Despite a large population and a large area, 70% of China's population lives in the coastal regions. This helps companies who look for markets access a relatively

small area with a dense population. Marketing of products in China is thus easier than say in India.

2. China is the most populous country in the world and after its economic liberalization has seen a fairly uniform and universal rise in the GDP. This prosperity of the Chinese, albeit moderate when compared to the US and Japan has nonetheless created enormous demand for real estate, automobiles, consumer durables and utilities such as electricity and various kinds of services.

3. Despite being the third largest country in the world in terms of territory of 9.5 million square kilometres, China has only 15 to 20% of arable land. The rest of the country is mountainous or is taken over by deserts. The land to man ratio in China is thus adverse and the tendency for people to migrate out of villages into the cities always remains.

4. China, due to its large desert and its openness to Siberia in the north is prone to environmental disasters whenever tree cover is sheered to make way for roads and high ways.

The above list tries to assess China as a country with the potential of a large consumer base. The above does not assess China as a country with the potential for generating growth and incomes for its people to emerge as consumers. For that one must turn towards some other kinds of observations made by T.J.Bond, Chief Economist, Merrill Lynch in 2002-03 with respect to the important linkages within China's economy.

Bond observes that China's decisions to expand capacities in its basic sectors like chemicals, transport equipment and base metals helped the growth and development of a slew of industries as backward linkages. The growths of employment in these industries helped labour earn wages that raised incomes and aspirations and thus propelled China's growth. But the divide in the industrial sector still prevailed as the industries around Shanghai and the Pearl River Delta tried to remain segregated from the enterprises of the mainland. In fact China attempted to emerge as two nations; the city driven model of high value and high growth and the inner area based production of small and cheap consumer goods. The capture of the basic commodity production by the centre starved China of its inputs of intermediate products and sparked off corruption in terms of smuggling of these commodities from the centre to the mainland.

What boggles the mind is that why did China attempt to create a purposeful divide between its regions and how could it attain such a mammoth growth despite that divide?

Actually China invested in some major industries which were financed by the FDI and FII; the opportunities of backward and forward linkages were also ensured to these FDIs and FIIs. The mammoth growth of China was supposed to be a haven for the foreign investors and the foreign investors had to be protected from the onslaught of cheaper goods produced in China's interior. Thus Communism, actually helped global capital prosper and smothered the local bases of production. Democracy, on the other had been more of a local assertion for participating in the market that Deng was so fervently pushing forth. The markets never really reached the people except as smuggled goods from the foreign companies where inflation sky rocketed. Employment in these production centres was well paid but scanty and uncertain and young people tried to save as much of their wages as they could. Real estate was the area in which people tried to invest in order to beat inflation. No wonder then the demand for real estate escalated.

A major difference between Deng and Mao was that Deng released the aspirational side of the farmers to retain their food surpluses and then invest the same to procure labour force and labour power to build infrastructure and manufacturing and service industries; but unlike Mao, Deng purposely impoverished the very same peasants when they set up their town and village enterprises and helped foreign investors to claim their field. Deng wanted to keep peasants in their fields so that they continued to remain producers of cheap food, the basic wage good. Mao forced surpluses out of peasants through communes; Deng manipulated the economy in a manner in which peasants were kept from emerging out of their fields. It was to maintain low food prices that Deng created the two Chinas. Communism helped maintain the stronghold of the Communist Party and reign in its cadets in the countryside while systematically denying the villages to extend their investments into manufacturing and services and keeping them confined to food production.

Observations from the banking sector are likely to vindicate the above thesis.

Today there are over 40,000 financial institutions in China

but the banks are controlled by four state owned units. These are namely the Agricultural Bank of China, China Construction Bank, Bank of China, and Industrial and Commercial Bank of China. These banks control nearly 70% of the aggregate assets of the financial institutions.

Interestingly, these banks have enormous outstanding loans nearly four times as that of their deposits. Keith Irving, the Regional Bank Analyst of Merrill Lynch observes that the outstanding loans in China by banks are four times that of Hong Kong's. Irving says that a possible reason for this anomaly is the lack of intermediation in the Chinese credit flow. This means that there is a deep divide between the community at large which generates the enormous savings as high as 60% of the GDP and the heap of outstanding loans of banks to parties who never seem to be producing wealth. The divide between the people and the State owned banks indicate that China seems to be fond of working with two systems; one of the state led, Party led China and the other of its people [86].

The above anomaly was generated mainly due to the fact that the State owned sector preferred foreign firms to the local domestic firms. These foreign firms did not perform as the State owned banking industry had expected it to. Since the local economy did not get the required credit, they did not wish to place their deposits in the banks. This produced the paradox of the accumulated savings on the one hand and the mountain of non-performing loans on the other.

---

[86] http://www.nytimes.com/1999/11/17/business/worldbusiness/17iht-chibank.2.t_0.html

But how China managed the mountain of non-performing loans is interesting. Around the years 2005 and 2006, China started speculating hugely in commodities. China was buying up iron ore, exporting coking coal, and consisted of half the world's stocks of nickel, zinc, aluminium and in short, every metal which is traded in the world. The decision of China to host the 2008 Olympics was a way of investing massively in infrastructure and construction projects awarded to foreign companies. While speculation earned for the Chinese billions of dollars, yet the collapse of economies all across the world left surpluses in hands of some major and influential Chinese firms and even individuals. China's militarism became an area of investing the monies. China supplies missiles to both Iraq and China, and the new interest in reopening up of the Silk Road has significant implications for militarization of the central Asia. The on-going tensions among the several nationalities along central Asia is a new area of not only desiring to strategically control these regions but given that these areas are also rich coal bearing blocks, control on these territories also means energy security.

If one was an investor looking for opportunities in China one could list out the following:

1. Investment in manufacturing was a good idea, especially if the unit was an outsourced business of a global chain. This is better than investing in smaller Chinese firms.

2. Chinese firms which employ sophisticated but indigenous technologies are likely to be more cost effective than outsourced firms which import technology.

The Chinese have little respect for patent rights and have no compunction in imitating designs and processes. Hence firms with imported technology are likely to have higher costs.

3. China's work force is ageing and because of the one child norm, China's labour replacement rate is low. Besides, wages are rising and the synergy between rural and urban regions made possible with China's family networks are declining due to low reproduction rate. Manufacturing may no longer be as lucrative as it used to be some time ago. The outsourced units are shifting to Bangladesh, Vietnam and Myanmar.

4. Investment in speculation is lucrative, especially in mineral resources. China has vast deposits of minerals and because of the bank runs always has money for investing in mineral speculation.

5. China is investing in infrastructure development, especially the railway network in its interior provinces; this is a good area to invest in.

6. The other profitable investment area is environment; China is plagued by environmental threats, and technologies in the management of the environment would do very well.

Chapter Twelve

Deng Xiaoping Versus China

Ruchir Sharma writes of the sustained economic growth of China between 1978 to 2002 that China could maintain such momentum was entirely due to the "Deng Dynasty"[87]. To the informed observer, it appears that Deng Xiaoping took over the reins of China and transformed it into the super power that it is. While such a view on the great visionary is legitimate, it is also true that China as a society played no less an important role in its own transformation as a super power. Deng and the Chinese society were often at loggerheads; sometimes one defied the other and at other times, one let the other be. Deng did not always lead China to its redemption; more often than not, they walked in parallel tracks.

Deng was born of a rural farming family in the province of Sichuan in China. A brilliant student, he won scholarships to study in the town beyond his village. Later he was among a handpicked set of Chinese students to win scholarships to France. When in France Deng discovered that the Chinese students were hoodwinked and instead of being allowed to study, they were made to work in factories. This was the

---

[87]Ruchir Sharma. Breakout Nations- In Pursuit if the Next Economic Miracles. Penguin. USA. 2012. Pg 29.

time of the WWI and most young men were conscripted as soldiers leaving factories largely empty of workforce. In a Chaplinesque manner, Deng found out the ways of the capitalists and took them as natural enemies of the society. He found inspiration in the French Socialist movements and also joined the Chinese students in France supporting the Communist Movement in China. Deng wrote a journal and was in charge of propaganda, and it was as if he, vicariously engendered China's Communist movement. Ezra Vogel observes very well that it was as if Deng was seeing the entire Communist movement as one who was creating it[88].

When Deng moved back to China, he like everyone else became a nationalist. This was in the year 1919, nationalism was the flavour of the youth and nationalism rather than communism formed the basis for Deng's consciousness. But when the split began to happen within the nationalists and the left wing Communists drifted away, Deng was moved by the Communist leader Mao's charisma. Not only charisma, but Deng was also impressed by the Soviet Union's development path. Deng was a student of Moscow during the days of the National Economic Programme (NEP) prior to the development of the Soviet model of economic growth. The NEP was closer to an ideal programme for China in which the local farmers and manufacturers remained while the State sponsored the heavy industries. Deng regarded the NEP to have worked very well; however later as the Soviet Union wholly nationalized the production system under its

---

[88] Ezra F. Vogel. Deng Xiaoping and The Transformation of China. Harvard University Press. USA. 2011. Pp 18-22.

heavy industries programme and led the world in science and technology, Deng seemed to find his ideals realized under the Soviet System. The Soviet system used the Western knowledge but unlike the capitalists did not pursue brute profits to the detriment of its workers and consumers. Hence state controlled industries appeared to be the best of both worlds for Deng. It is pertinent to note that before Deng went to the Soviet Union, he had been sent in a student's exchange programme to France, also a socialist country albeit under the format of liberal democracy. Deng experienced a sham socialism in the country steeped with exploitation of labour and racism and callous towards the poor; this experience made him to disbelieve in liberal democracy as ever serving the cause of socialism[89].

Deng Xiaoping seemed to always have a penchant for organizing movements and implementing programmes. During the Long March of Mao Zedong, Deng was posted in the rural areas of south Western China. In the long period between 1930 and 1937, Deng experienced that the rural folk were divided, competitive, and envious of one another, small minded, petty and back biting and that Communism was often a tool for wielding power, and witch hunt potential threats to one's schemes. Deng's mistrust for the rural folk and the local leaders of Communism later manifested in his open discrimination against interior China when he directed his favours to the Blue water areas of the coastal and more urbanized China like Shanghai during the opening up of the economy.

---

[89]Ibid. Pp 266-310

However, in 1937 when the Japanese attacked China, the nationalists and the communists came together under the nationalist banner. Everyone was in arms to defend China in a nationalist spirit. Deng did very well in this military assignment and emerged in a position of command. Later when we observe the "Deng years" in China we realize that between 1978 and 1991, Deng was able together a network of influence which was related to investments but mired in military and defence concerns. Deng also seemed to have understood military strategy very well because in the aftermath of the Vietnam War, he was able to arouse the defeated spirits of the US into investing in South East Asia, Korea and Hong Kong and Taiwan and contain the rising aggression of the Soviet Union especially in Laos and to an extent in Malaysia. China's rise as a regional power which assured investors of returns on capital if they poured money in China, a country which is still Communist and does not have institutions which the West would consider as being appropriate to the market.

Between 1946 and 1949, civil war between the nationalists and the communists broke out in China. Deng was now the highest ranking official of the Communist Party and was in charge of the provinces in the east, namely Shangdong, Hebei, Henan and Shanxi. These provinces were better off than Sichuan, his native province in terms of economy and education and it is here Deng was to raise his Communist army. While recruiting for military, Deng disregarded the family connections and social networks which some families seemed to have attained out of Communism; instead he relied on merit and individual talent. For Deng, Communism had created new forms of power structures and whenever he emerged in any position of power tended to disregard Communism in the villages and small towns. Deng, believed in Communism as State control over resources and as a centralized command of the State over the society. This was to underlie his open disregard for the Town and Village Enterprises, his mistrust of piles of rural savings and his utter surprise when the farmers of China fuelled the engine of growth rather than the large State owned Enterprises which Deng supported. In his active regionalism, we watched how Deng openly discriminated in favour of large capital and disfavoured the rural based enterprises as cheap and unethical imitators of brands especially the electronic products.

In the years of laying the foundation for the Communist rule, between 1952 and 1959, it is again Deng who designed the Maoist programme. It was he who implemented the agricultural cooperatives, fixed grain quotas and built handicraft collectives. Liu Shaoqui designed the programmes and Deng tried to implement the same as per the letter. However, he realized that not every province was the same and that economies varied within China; while in the eastern provinces of wet cultivation, cooperatives and collectivization were easier than in the western and northern provinces where land was arid and vast and thus unsuitable for intensive cropping. In these years, Deng realized that one size could not possibly fit all and when Mao allowed criticisms against his programme to flow in under the "Let Hundred Flowers Bloom" programme Deng criticized Mao's collectivization the most. Deng's pragmatism cost him his career in the Party as well as in the Government, his family was harassed, his son paralyzed and he was exiled away in a remote village[90].

Later on, as Deng comes back in power in 1978, under the Chairmanship of Hu Yaobang, Deng dissolves collectives and instates the household responsibility system where farmers could retain their surpluses. The Anhui experiment in which few farmers used their surpluses to barter goods among themselves and send their children to cities, albeit totally against the law, motivated Deng to dissolve grain quotas and revert surpluses back to farmers[91]. In fact, it was in the Anhui province where Deng takes note of the illegal migrants fleeing to Hong Kong and decides to legalize migration into Hong Kong and open up China's economy into a greater trade with the former. Much of Deng's motivation to build relations with Hong Kong comes from the Anhui events, both to restore surpluses to farmers as well as to integrate the economy of China into that of Hong Kong even if it be as a supplier of labour. Besides, Deng Xiaoping was no different from any other Chinese who lived on the old Qing glory and resolved to restore China to the pre Opium War days and the return of Hong Kong from the British was a part of this restoration[92].

---

[90] Ibid. Pp 91-119

[91] Ted C Fishman. China Inc -The Relentless Rise of the Next Superpower. Simon and Schuster. London. 2005. Pp 46-49.

[92] "China has sought that wealth and power as a way of gaining supremacy in what was to China the entire known world. China's vision kept it at the centre of the world (the translation of the Chinese term for "China" literally means "Middle Kingdom"), with all of the states on its periphery paying tribute to China's rulers in much the same way that vassals paid tribute to Europeans or Japan feudal lords". In Richard Bernstein and Ross.H.Munro. The Coming Conflict With China. Vintage. USA. 1987. Pg 53.

Deng was a Communist because he hated the profit motive in capitalism, but he maintained a form faith in the nationalist policy of science and technology and industry. For Deng, an active pursuit of modern science was a priority. He invited Chinese scientists and intellectuals back in China, invited investments from political enemies like Japan and Korea to invest in high end industries like metals and chemicals and automobiles in China. Deng backed his open door policy in investments by posturing the military strength of his country in South East Asia and Korea. Militarism seemed natural to Deng, perhaps also due to the nationalist which lay dormant within his Communist self. Like a nationalist, Deng wanted to absorb Taiwan within China, the seat of nationalist power. Like the nationalists, Deng believed more in heavy industry, presence in the seas, free citizens rather than Communist teams.

Yet, for Deng the rule of the Central Party was very important. Deng was also an elitist, one who had little faith in the villagers doing commerce among them and producing cheap goods for the world to become the engine of super growth of a super nation that China aspired to become. He did not seem to believe in rebellion and also because he associated rebellions too much to the wild tribes, or to the unschooled peasants emerging from the outer areas into the civilized centres of the country. This perhaps explains why despite being exiled, having lost his first wife and child to the Revolution, the torture of his children by the Party and on one occasion, his second wife turning against him and turning him in as a "rightist", Deng never rebelled against the Party.

When we observe Deng's admiration for the Chinese intellectuals educated abroad, especially the United States, and his pursuit of market freedom, his role in causing the Tiananmen Tragedy that had the military roll out and crush a peaceful demonstration by students who were charged with ideas of individual freedom, is an anomaly. Only Deng's unshakeable faith in the Communist Party could explain this. Deng neither allowed the local village level and provincial leaders to get the better of the Central Command nor did he allow the western educated intellectuals to run the State.

Both Mao and Deng looked towards a new China. For Mao, a new China would mean a cutting off of all traditional ties like bonds of the family, worship of ancestors, cosseting of children and village gossip circles. Instead, men and women should view themselves as members of the Communist Party. For Deng, traditional ties were not so much of a problem but he wanted that men and women must be committed nationalists and patriots and rise above local bickering and pettiness. Analysts seem to believe that it was Deng through a slew of neo liberal and market based economic policies made China into a superpower. It is being suggested here that it was not Deng alone who brought about the change; instead it were the millions of Chinese people who because of their innate character created by a unique history emerged as entrepreneurs, traders, and very quick learners to displace efficient labour force of Hong Kong and Taiwan. Were this innate entrepreneurship not there in China, no amount of market friendly policies could have worked.

While working out market friendly policies Deng seemed

to have relied on exports, military presence, and foreign direct investments and advancing easy loans. But observed closely, these policies did not seem to take Deng very far. Banks accumulated non-performing assets with loans which were never paid back; the State owned enterprises, despite granting freedom of decision making to managers continued to remain unprofitable and most exports from China were cheap only because not all costs were accounted for. What then made these reforms work lay elsewhere; they lay in the Chinese society. The Chinese people by producing, trading, investing and absorbing the costs of education, nutrition and health among the family members created an economic density upon which emerged China into a super economy. China's growth did not lie in its policies; they lay in Deng's pragmatism in allowing the Chinese to be what they naturally and innately are, materialistic, self-interested, motivated, competitive, and envious, hankering after social prestige, ostentatious and practical.

The savings rates in China are very high and people do not encourage consumption through borrowings. In fact the high rate of savings in China became a problem for Deng. Deng's liberalization of banks was a means to access the vast deposits of household savings for the State owned enterprises and away from the local enterprises, the last of which was repulsive to Deng. It is therefore more likely that the investors went to China for its cheap and highly skilled labour force, it's easy labour laws, its corruptible officials where one could bribe one's way through, the lose environmental laws which allowed mindless exploitation of mineral resources, its abundant natural resources, the access to the entire Pacific and Indian Ocean through the South China seas, its large speculative base for iron ore and coal and other metals like nickel, zinc, lead and copper and the scope for investing money as most sectors are open to the FDI.

Chapter Thirteen

What Drove China's Growth - Some Possible Explanations

It is time for us to reflect upon our main question with which we started the book, how was it possible for China to grow to such enormous heights of economic power. It is usual for scholars to assign the high growth of China to the openness of trade, openness to foreign competition and other related neo liberal policies of freeing rates of interests in banks, reducing tariffs and discarding protection for labour. The above policies helped opening up the Chinese economy and creating in it vents to use the innate Chinese talents. But these policies were designed also to accommodate the foreign investments into China that brought along with it new technologies, new capital, new markets and new visions. Scholars have vied with one another in order to isolate exactly those causes that made China grow so fast and for so long; scholars have also tried to assess the various shortcomings in the path of China's growth in order to set a time for the arrest and decline of the growth.

Linda Yueh in her magnificent work on China attempts to evaluate the parameters of the neoclassical economics in the possible role that they have played in the growth story[93]. In this story she shows that institutions such as democracy, property rights, and legal institutions supporting the market, patent laws, stock exchange, and the various banking systems are actually pretty much out of place. There does not seem to be any exceptional accumulation of physical, financial or human capital; besides, the Chinese story is a mix of layoffs and informalization of the industrial sector belying the thesis that growth in the country has taken place due to capital accumulation. But in her detailed examination of the various econometric models and surveys undertaken by economists across the world based on firm panel data, she seems to veer towards the factor that this book seems to suggest so far and which is social capital that exists as a network of peers, colleagues, neighbours, alumni and extended family and kinship known as Guanxi in the Chinese language. It is this human network that multiplies gains to investments; it helps entrepreneurs secure credit, access markets, procure raw materials and in entering into a chain of cooperation in the process of production. The human agglomerates in the form of the Guanxi helps sustain a knowledge economy which can help in the acquiring of technological skills. Yueh mentions that of the many factors considered and then rejected as having made the Chinese miracle possible, foreign collaborations seemed to have worked the best; these foreign firms brought with them technology that were quickly replicated and reproduced in China in its small and informal

---

[93]Linda Yueh, China's Growth - The Making of an Economic Superpower. OUP. Great Britain. 2012.

factories more often set up by groups of friends or societies of relatives and fellow villagers and helped by China's openness and the large non-resident relative connection occupy shelves in New York, London and Paris. What Yueh does not mention is the fact that so much of this non-farm manufacturing was supported by the farming families who provided for the workers while they set up shops and factories, took time to learn skills and eventually start the production lines. The family seems to be the very institution which helped China initiate and sustain its growth.

Khalid Malik in his work on China is more articulate in his criticisms of the neo classical paradigm in explaining economic growth[94]. Like Yueh, Malik too trashes theories of factor accumulation, factor reallocation, human capital and total factor productivity and like Yueh he too is confounded by the fact that while openness of the economy may be a necessary explanation for the sudden spurt of economic activities it is not a sufficient condition. Unlike Yueh, Malik does not agree that foreign collaborations had something to do with the economic miracles and instead he agrees that China had been growing for over a decade prior to the liberalization of foreign investments. Malik says that contrary to the theories of economic growth, privatization with informalization actually helped China grow and to sustain that growth. Malik like Yueh, through a process of elimination agrees to the fact that the social capital namely Guanxi made all the difference. The social networks helped entrepreneurs survive and sustain the

---

[94]Khalid Malik, Why Has China Grown So Fast For So Long? OUP. Delhi. 2012.

unbelievable economic growth.

Pranab Bardhan's work on China and India is again rather inconclusive for he finds nothing by way of neo liberal policies to explain China's growth[95]. Neither savings nor investments, neither banks nor bonds, neither regional integration nor regional isolation, neither decentralization nor central command seem to explain the Chinese growth. There has not been exceptionally high savings nor exceptionally cheap bank lending and access to finance from banks have been rather limited; there has been regional implosion of economies as local powers have held strong control over the town and village industries and the urban centres have had very little security of employment. Privatization is no answer because China started to grow much before the drive for privatization; in fact a lot of Chinese growth seems to correspond with high labour retrenchment from the state sector when train loads of workers were sent back to their homes in the villages. These workers trooped and revived the Town and Village industries which were the backbone of the Chinese resurrection all through the 1980's. And this was possible because Deng had allowed the farmers to retain their farm surpluses and which not only gave them to produce more but with this increased production they could support the large non-farm workers in their endeavours to collectively restart the town and village enterprises. The start of the Chinese miracle may be the return of the ownership of the farm surplus to the farmers even though farms continued

---

[95]Pranab Bardhan, Awakening Giants - Feet of Clay. Assessing the Economic Rise of China and India. OUP. Delhi. 2010.

to be owned collectively.   Once again, inadvertently and unknowingly, Pranab Bardhan identifies the social network at work in China.

While the above thesis of the social network or the Guanxi can explain how China grew so fast and strong because it was the Guanxi that helped the absorption of foreign technology, getting on to a higher knowledge curve and engendering a learning society, the Guanxi is inadequate to explain the gigantic volume of the Chinese growth to command over half of the global economy, its holding of a lion's share of the US debt, its investments in almost every country of the world. For this we must understand yet another dimension of the Chinese mind and which is to always emerge as the most important nation on earth, or the Middle Kingdom. China's growth also stems from the Chinese imagination and commitment to be the most powerful nation upon earth to which every other nation is only a subservient obeisance payer. The discipline of economics is so centred around the rational decision maker who is an individual that it completely eliminates forms of behaviour of economic agent which have a collective spirit. The Chinese is an individual when she is committed to earning wealth but she is equally a team player when she aligns her actions to the larger national goals which secure for her even larger opportunities. The Chinese are individual players and respond immensely well to demands for coordinated actions. Such coordination is best observed in the Chinese behaviour in international trade.

Once a Chinese finds a way to export his wares to a country, the next step for him would be to find avenues in which he can invest his export earnings into the very same country. The Chinese uses the trade surplus to invest in the importing sectors of the importing country. The Chinese piggyback rides on the shoulders of nations like South Korea, Japan and the USA and access their export markets. Eric J Weiner traces how the Chinese enterprises seem to invest in the US firms which are engaged in the buying of the Chinese products[96]. China imported minerals especially iron ore from Rio Tinto in order to make steel; it exports finished steel to Brazil and Australia, the very sources of import of iron ore and uses the proceeds to buy up mineral properties in these countries. In India, China buys up iron ore with the proceeds its earns from exporting coal to the country and in the aftermath of the limits on iron ore production, China is investing in pellet making facilities in order to source pellets for export to China. The Chinese operate on both sides of the border; they are at once exporters and importers. This is why once the Chinese are into an economy they become intrinsic players in the businesses of the partner countries. This strategic act of the Chinese has been mentioned only in passing and more in a manner of being inferred from a host of references. Weiner seems to be more concerned with the corporate espionage of the Chinese into the US firms and insider trading of stocks and bonds. But he does not seem to realize why this is done; the Chinese use trade to integrate the economies, much like it did under the Song and the Tang dynasties. This has been a historical pattern and for China, histories are to be repeated.

---

[96]Eric J Weiner, The Shadow Market How The Sovereign Wealth Finds Secretly Dominate The Global Economy, Oneworld. Great Britain. 2010.

Dambisa Moyo in her recent book mentions how the Chinese are gobbling up natural resources across the world. She seems to be especially scandalized at the Chinese proposition to buy up an entire hill containing copper in Peru![97] But she does not seem to ask herself why does China need such large swathes of natural resources so as to forage in Africa for arable land, dig up the Dead Sea for potash, militarise Central Asia for salt? Is it only to feed its own population which is now stable but on the way to decline? No, China wants to control the production of every commodity in the world and which is why it seeks to control the means to those productions which are the raw materials. China's ambition is to be able to control every production facility in the world and for this it would need all the raw materials of the world as well.

Scholars have been foxed by China not being a democracy and yet could pull off an economic miracle. Once again we are caught up with theories those are founded upon the histories of capitalism in the West imagining that in every case of capitalist growth, societies also must be preceded by democracies. This is hardly true and Ruchir Sharma identifies authoritarian regimes such as Indonesia, Myanmar, Kazakhstan and Russia have sustained over 10% growth in recent times. India being the world's largest democracy has hardly helped it grow to such economic heights[98]. However, to merely say that authoritarian regimes are as good for

---

[97]Dambisa Moyo. Winner Takes All- China's Race For Resources and What It Means for the US. Penguin. UK. 2012.

[98]Ruchir Sharma. Breakout Nations - In Pursuit of the Next Economic Miracle. Penguin. UK. 2012. pg 30.

economic growth as democracies are is to miss out the real connection between political regimes and economic growth. China's Communism was very well suited to pull off the economic miracle because it was the best suited to the Chinese society especially to redeem the Chinese world view; Mao made a mistake of aligning too closely to the Soviet system, while Deng reset it to suit the innate Chinese mentality.

The discourses of the day have moved slightly away from the difficulties of explaining China's economic growth and instead seem to focus on the forecast how long can the growth last. Such discussions invariably lead us to another blind alley because if we have not really concluded why the growth was possible in the first place, it will be difficult to assess when the forces will taper off. Nonetheless, theories of tapering off China's growth emanate from two sources; one seeks to explain that China's economy has already reached the peak and it is only natural that whatever goes up will come down again. China's costs are rising and thus taking away the advantage of cheap goods and besides the recession in the USA and the EU, the world's largest markets and the cooling off of India because of the rupee free fall are capping the demand for the Chinese goods. The other explanation is sociological and pertains to demography. China's one child norm is now showing in a slowdown in population growth and enormous inheritance for the child in the family from as many as six to twelve adults that leave China at the mercy of pampered boys who are reluctant to work. Besides, the economic growth albeit based out of a manufacturing sector and the consequent urbanization proliferated into the growth of the service sector. Incidentally, the service sector, while a commendable cauldron for absorbing the unemployed or the self-employed, it is also a sector where wages grow ahead of labour productivity; growth which is dominated by the services are likely to be inflationary. Besides, the fast rise of wages in the service sector destroys the focus, concentration and the morale of those employed in the manufacturing sector where a rise in wages depends upon a rise in labour productivity.

Labour increasingly shifts from manufacturing into services and while factories might have vacancies, not many are willing to take up such jobs and are even less willing to go through the grind of acquiring the required skills. Tendencies as the above usually destroy the manufacturing base of the economy and hence the Chinese investors are today fritting across the globe in search of societies with good manufacturing skills in which to locate their businesses. China is investing in the manufacturing sectors of Brazil and South Africa, in Liberia and Morocco, in Turkmenistan and Kirghizia. Ruchir Sharma insists that China's labour supply is falling; its youth waning and soon its goods sector will thin out too leading China into high inflation, high wage and high unemployment economy[99].

Lee Kuan Yew says that China's growth may only be capped by the total availability of raw materials in the world; there was a time when China was the most powerful Empire in the known world; today things have changed. China has to work in tandem with the national interests of so many

---

[99]Ibid. pg 22.

countries[100]. Access to raw materials might be limited for China, limiting its growth. Today the Chinese are becoming rather reluctant to invest in mineral properties in view of the rising prices, a phenomenon caused by the Chinese demand; this reluctance stems from the fact that the scope of prices rising in the future are limited and the Chinese do not seem to be aware of buyers of their natural resource property as speculative investments. The world is still too enamoured of China to worry about the possible decline in its economic might; China today drives the growth engine for the world and the loss of China will be akin to the driver abandoning the vehicle leaving passengers stranded in the middle of nowhere.

Khalid Malik raises the issue of sustainability of the Chinese growth in view of the environmental issues[101]. The Chinese government has already banned iron ore mining and coal mining in various locations in China and placed restrictions on steel production and aluminium processing in view of the pollution. Malik mentions how China is totally reinventing itself in its energy basket going towards every conceivable kind of renewable energy solar, wind and geothermal. Indeed, what Malik seems to have missed and even Moyo (2012)[102] does not mention is the fact that China's incursion into the economies of Africa, Latin America and Central Asia is as much to access the natural resources like sunshine, water, strong winds and geothermal energies as it is to access platinum, uranium and copper.

[100]Lee Kuan Yew. Op cit 2 pg 9

[101]Khalid Malik,Why Has China Grown So Fast for So Long, OUP, India 2012, pg 220

[102]Dambisa Moyo, op cit 91

China's growth has been directed at world conquest; China's growth must also be sustained with that vision.

Supplementary Readings:

1. C. Fred Bergsten, Bates Gill, Nicholas Lardy and Derek Mitchell. China, The Balance Sheet - What the World Needs to Know About The Emerging Superpower. Public Affairs. New York. 2007.

2. Laurence. J. Brahm. China's Century - The Awakening of the Next Economic Powerhouse. John Wiley and Sons PTE ltd. Singapore. 2001.

3. Ted C Fishman. China Inc - How The Rise of the Next Superpower Challenges America and the West. Simon and Schuster Uk Ltd. Africa House. London. 2005.

4. Immanuel C.Y.Hsu. The Rise of Modern China. OUP. New York. 2000.

5. Tarun Khanna. Billions of Entrepreneurs - How China and India Are Reshaping Their Futures and Yours. Barnes and Nobles. Harvard Business Review. USA. 2007.

6. Mark Leonard. What Does China Think? Harper Collins. London. 2006.

7. Jonathan Mirsky. Modern China. Britannica Guide. London. 2008.

8. Randall Prerenboom. China Modernizes. OUP. New York. 2007.

9. John Bryan Starr. Understanding China - A Guide to China's Economics, History and Political Culture. Hill and Wang. New York. 1997.

10. Joe Studwell. The China Dream- The Elusive Quest For The Greatest Untapped Market in the World. Profile Books. London. 2004.

11. Jeffrey. N.Wasserstrom. China in the 21st Century - What Everyone Needs to Know. OUP. New York. 2010.